HOPE
when it's hard

Copyright © 2026 by Nancy Jo Gibson

All rights reserved.
No part of this book may be reproduced in any form without written permission from the publisher.

ISBN: 979-8-9906278-3-5

Unless otherwise noted, scripture quotations are taken from the Holy Bible, New Living Translation, copyright © 1996, 2004, 2015 by Tyndale House Foundation. Used by permission of Tyndale House Publishers, Carol Stream, Illinois 60188. All rights reserved.

Scripture quotations marked ESV are taken from The ESV® Bible ("The Holy Bible, English Standard Version®), copyright © 2001 by Crossway, a publishing ministry of Good News Publishers. Used by permission. All rights reserved.

Scripture quotations marked KJV are taken from The Authorized (King James) Version. Rights in the Authorized Version in the United Kingdom are vested in the Crown. Reproduced by permission of the Crown's patentee, Cambridge University Press.

Scripture quotations marked NIV are taken from The Holy Bible, New International Version® NIV® Copyright © 1973, 1978, 1984, 2011 by Biblica, Inc. Used with permission. All rights reserved worldwide.

Scripture quotations marked NASB are taken from the New American Standard Bible®, Copyright © 1960, 1971, 1977, 1995, 2020 by The Lockman Foundation. Used by permission. All rights reserved. www.Lockman.org.

Scripture quotations marked TPT are from The Passion Translation®. Copyright © 2017, 2018, 2020 by Passion & Fire Ministries, Inc. Used by permission. All rights reserved. ThePassionTranslation.com.

Scripture quotations marked NLV are taken from the New Life Version, Copyright © 1969 and 2003. Used by permission of Barbour Publishing, Inc., Uhrichsville, Ohio 44683. All rights reserved.

Published by Hillside Publishing
P.O. Box 907
Fishersville, VA 22939
hillside-publishing.com

HOPE
when it's hard

Finding the Light in the
Darkest Seasons of Life

NANCY JO GIBSON

HILLSIDE
PUBLISHING

I waited patiently for the Lord to help me,
and he turned to me and heard my cry.
He lifted me out of the pit of despair,
out of the mud and the mire.
He set my feet on solid ground
and steadied me as I walked along.
He has given me a new song to sing,
a hymn of praise to our God.

Psalm 40:1–3a

Table of Contents

Foreword 11

Preface 13

I. Trust

Chapter 1: Hoping For vs. Hoping In 16
Chapter 2: Hope Anchored in Trust 24
Chapter 3: Relationship That Builds Trust 29
Chapter 4: God's Will & God's Promises 40
Chapter 5: Trust Him 48

II. Truths

Chapter 6: God Goes Before Us 51
Chapter 7: God Walks With Us 57
Chapter 8: God Follows After Us 64

III. Trapped

Chapter 9: In the Pit of Despair 71
Chapter 10: When You Can't See God 78

IV. Trouble

Chapter 11: Hope After Failure 108
Chapter 12: A Famous Fall from Grace 114

Chapter 13: Out of Hopelessness   125
Chapter 14: Lament   134
Chapter 15: Grace After Grief   140
Chapter 16: No Condemnation   151

V. Transformed

Chapter 17: Evidence of His Presence   158
Chapter 18: Humility   168
Chapter 19: Openness   179
Chapter 20: Presence   188
Chapter 21: Encouragement   195

VI. Triumph

Chapter 22: Our Choice   204
Chapter 23: The Pathway to Peace   209

Epilogue   216

Extras

"Hope-Full" Scriptures   222
Songs of Hope   238
Holding Hope in the Silence   241
Recommended Reading   244

Foreword

There she was! Coming through the doors of our church foyer, herding two active little boys and holding tightly to a squirming little girl with curly hair. Her voice was soft but firm, with just a hint of pride, as she guided them through the maze of people standing there. Her husband was pushing through too, carrying her purse, a Bible, a diaper bag, and a cup of coffee.

This is my first memory of Nancy Jo Gibson and her family. Little did I know on that day that she would become one of my dearest friends, a prayer partner, and someone who would infinitely affect my life forever. We would share a thousand cups of tea, hilarious laughter, and moments of intense grief. And I have been blessed to know this gifted woman for over forty years and to have her call me "Mom." The Lord knew I needed to know her.

During fifteen years as a client advocate at a crisis pregnancy center, I met hundreds of young women who felt hopeless in very difficult situations. So when I learned that Nancy Jo was writing a book—*Hope When It's Hard*—I immediately knew that no one could offer hope better than she to all of us who hurt.

As you delve into these pages, you will come to understand

that she has every reason to be devoid of hope. Yet she wrote this book to help you and me find that very thing.

Hope — it's illusive and intangible, but as necessary to us as breathing. Nancy Jo affirms this in every page of the book you now hold in your hands. She allows her vulnerability, personal reflection, and profound knowledge of relevant Scriptures to shine forth in ways that offer practical, useful, trustworthy wisdom to truly hope when it's hard.

In her various roles as wife, mother, daughter, friend, and Director of Soul Care and Biblical Guidance at Church on the Hill in Fishersville, Virginia (now retired), Nancy Jo has honed her skills to counsel and be a source of encouragement and healing to countless men and women, many of them without hope.

Most importantly, Nancy Jo *always* points to Jesus! As an example, here is an excerpt from Chapter 4: "The choice is this: Do I go through life, which will be terribly difficult at times, with or without Jesus?"

Hurt is hard! And hope is hard work. As you begin this book, read it expectantly, prayerfully, and thoughtfully. You are about to embark on a beautiful journey . . . a journey leading to Hope!

—Betty Herron Lambert

ENDORSEMENTS

"*Hope When It's Hard* is both profoundly personal and deeply scriptural—a lifeline for those navigating sorrow, disappointment, or even wounds of their own making. With rare tenderness and uncompromising truthfulness, Nancy Jo Gibson refuses to gloss over suffering. Instead, she bears witness to the God who meets us in the depths, whose presence, mercy, and transforming power reach further than any pit. Through its pages, readers are invited into practices of trust, humility, lament, and gratitude—habits that, over time, reshape despair into something greater: a resilient hope rooted in God's faithfulness."

—DR. ANDREW WILLIAMS, *author of* Reconstructing Prayer *and* The Stories That Make Us

"Nancy Jo Gibson weaves a resilient thread of hope through deeply personal and painful stories, including the murder of her daughter, Rebekah. With remarkable honesty, that thread remains tethered to the loving heart of God, revealed again and again through Scripture. The result is a strengthening patchwork for the worn and weary reader—those who want to trust God but aren't sure how to do so in the midst of real pain. This is not a book of easy answers, but of God's faithful presence."

—JIM COOPER JR., *author of* Drowning in Drama: Jonah and the Drama Triangle

"We are certainly living in a hurting world. Almost every day we hear about (or may be close to) personal conflicts, life-threatening physical afflictions, marital strife, or ugly verbal encounters. Nancy Jo has experienced a heavy dose of hurtful situations in her life, especially in the tragic death of her daughter, but she has learned to live in hope. Her new book, *Hope When It's Hard*, does not sugarcoat the harsh realities of pains we all might live with. Instead, the book points us to biblical hope (even in hard times) with many practical words of sound advice. This book, with a strong emphasis on the Word of God itself, ought to lift up the heavy heart of anyone living with disappointments or unanswered questions. As you read, may you discover a new and living hope, centered in Jesus Christ, which will revitalize your life."

—CLAY STERRETT, *pastor (retired)*

"In *Hope When It's Hard*, Nancy Jo Gibson serves as a seasoned guide walking readers through the labyrinth of loss and pain into a broad place of hope. Conversational in style, her writing is personal without being maudlin, biblical without being preachy, hopeful without being trivializing. Through her own experiences, insight from Scripture, and drawing from the wisdom of others, Nancy Jo gently leads readers to a place of discovering beauty even amongst the ashes of life's most painful circumstances."

—BRANDON WILLIAMS, *pastor*

Preface

Hope!

The definition of *hope*, according to Merriam-Webster, is "to cherish a desire with anticipation: to want something to happen or be true."

Hope is a verb; that is, it is something we do. Examples given are "hopes for a promotion" or "hoping for the best."

We hope for innumerable things every day: *I hope it doesn't rain. I hope I get a good parking spot. I hope I'm not getting sick.* Sometimes we verbalize our hopes to ourselves and others, and sometimes we don't even realize we were actively hoping for something until it doesn't happen and we experience disappointment or sadness.

Hope is also a noun: "something hoped for," such as "great hopes for the coming year." But because *hoped* is in the definition, we must understand the verb—the action of having hoped—first.

Followers of Christ enjoy a deeper definition of *hope*, such as this one from retired pastor Clay Sterrett: "Hope is the continual expectation of good — a settled confidence that God has good plans for our future."

Hope is easy, natural, and even automatic in the general sense of the word. But there are times in life when it can be extremely difficult to have hope. Those are the times that I'm praying this little book will speak to. Times when hope is hard. When hope is out of reach. When troubles rear up like Godzilla, roaring loud enough to shake us to the core, spewing nasty spittle, and causing the spark of hope to flicker within the turmoil of our souls.

What do we do then? When the diagnosis comes in. When we get that phone call. When our marriage fails. When our children make destructive choices. When addiction strikes with ferocity. When we find ourselves stuck in a relentless, exhausting job with no way out, or when we lose our only source of income. When we are betrayed. When a loved one dies.

These circumstances that can crush our hope are countless. And we will most certainly all be affected by some of them in our lifetime. So! It would be good to have a plan in place. Some way to tether us to a true, genuine hope that can survive the tsunamis that are a given part of living in a fallen world.

I'm inviting you to join me in embracing and nurturing a hope that will strengthen us and carry us . . . a hope that is alive enough to become a force within us that propels us forward through even the most difficult of times!

I.
Trust

Chapter 1
Hoping For vs. Hoping In

In my first book, *Safe in Your Arms*, I related a little story about my children that I've often thought perfectly illustrates the two kinds of hope:

> One winter evening when the children were young (I'm guessing Davy was nine, Joseph seven, and Rebekah five), I had to drive the four of us to church in my husband's truck. We were all squished together in the front row, which was stuck in position for David's six-foot body, which did not suit my five-foot-three frame well. It was raining, and the defroster wasn't working. I was sitting on the edge of the seat, straining to reach the pedals and peering at the dark road through the diminishing spot of clear glass on the windshield.
>
> We had gotten about two-thirds of the way there when Joseph said, "Mommy, my tummy hurts."
>
> "Joseph, I'm sorry your tummy hurts," I responded. "Do you know why it's hurting?"
>
> "No," he said, which was followed by Davy's emphatic "I know why it's hurting! It's because you're afraid!"

What a blow to my ego! My driving wasn't that bad.

Joseph countered, "I'm not afraid."

Davy: "Well, you ought to be!"

Joseph: "Well, I'm not!" And just as I was ready to thank him for not doubting me and my driving skills, he continued: "I've already prayed about it, and if we all die, it's God's will."

I love this story! Those who hear it and know my sons as grown men can still see those same personalities shining through their full beards. But let's take a close look at how this story relates to hope.

It is vital for us to understand that there is a huge distinction between hoping *for* something and hoping *in* something. That winter evening, we were all hoping *for* the same thing: to arrive at church safely. The difference between Davy and Joseph was *who* they were hoping *in*.

Davy's hope was in Mommy—in my human ability to get us to church safely. He was anxious and fearful. And to be fair, the circumstances justified his fear (even though I was and honestly still am a pretty good driver). Joseph's hope was in God, trusting that one way or the other, God would take care of us. And what did he experience? Peace!

Let's take it a step further. I can't help but think of our recent (2024) presidential election. Can you remember where you put your hope? Was it anchored in God and knowing that no matter what the outcome of the election was, God would be with you and that His plans and purposes always prevail? Or was it in a certain candidate/political party? If the latter, I can pretty much guarantee that you, like the vast majority of the United

States, experienced a decent amount of fear and anxiety, just as little Davy did when his hope was in me.

But now go back and look closely at Davy's response to Joseph when Joseph said he was not afraid. "You ought to be," he said.

I realize that you are reading this, but I so wish I could tell you this story in person so you could hear me imitate Davy's indignation and utter disgust for his little brother's failure to see the situation the same way he did. When we put our hope in things or people, and others disagree with us, we feel threatened. They are not only disagreeing with us, but they are also threatening our desired outcome.

If, on the other hand, our hope is in God—His unfailing promises/character/provision—someone disagreeing with us does not threaten us in this way. We can join with Joseph and say, "You know, I've prayed about this, and I'm going to trust that God is going to take care of me one way or the other."

Whereas hoping for a desired outcome is natural, it's not always easy to hope so confidently in something that it brings the kind of peace that Joseph had.

Believe me, I know.

On January 28, 2009, our beloved daughter, Rebekah, was brutally murdered in Buckhannon, West Virginia. She was only twenty years old.

We had been through several years of rebellion, Rebekah bucking against us, her parents, and our rules, as well as delving into promiscuity, drugs, and alcohol. As a very compliant child myself, I genuinely had no idea how to handle a strong-willed child. I made many things absolutes that did not need to be, and I was overly strict and controlling. To make matters worse, when Rebekah made wrong choices, I tended to withdraw, not wanting to give the illusion of "supporting" her choices. In reality, I withdrew the evidence of my love that she desperately needed.

I certainly had hope that she would change, and in some ways, she did. She deeply longed to make good choices and to stay on a good, stable path. But in all honesty, my hope was either in her changing or in God removing certain influences from her life. I truly did not understand the difference between hoping in and hoping for, and this placed me on an emotional roller-coaster ride as our daughter vacillated between making better choices and being drawn back into a destructive lifestyle.

I in no way mean to imply that if I had only understood that I needed to place my hope in God, things would have been smooth sailing. Absolutely not! There still would have been much heartache and sorrow. However, I do believe that such understanding would have kept me from plunging into the depths of despair, as Anne of Green Gables would say. It would have also helped me hopefully surrender my desperate attempts to control and manipulate situations and people. And perhaps I could have stopped trying to dictate to God how He needed to handle things![1]

On January 28, 2009, all my hopes for Rebekah were crushed. At least it seemed so for a while. But God—ever gracious and

---

1. These lessons, as well as Rebekah's story, are covered in much greater detail in my first book, *Safe in Your Arms: A Daughter's Murder—A Mother's Forgiveness*.

merciful, even to "a wretch like me"—was who He always is: faithful, compassionate, merciful, gentle, forgiving. My Provider, Giver of Good Gifts, and Redeemer.

It is mostly from walking through devastating sorrow and deep regrets that I have changed from the inside out. And my husband and children would agree that these changes have been for the better!

I have learned many lessons as I journeyed through grief. One of the most important, I believe, has been recognizing the difference between hoping for and hoping in and how we can hold on to hope when we know (that we know that we know!) we can hope *in* God.

In the months after Rebekah's death, I was fixated on justice. I constantly prayed for justice to be done in a trial that kept being postponed. Every verse in the Psalms about justice was underlined and highlighted in my Bible. I agonized over the thought that Rebekah's murderer would not have to "pay" or "pay adequately" for what he did to our daughter. I detested the defense attorney who had the nerve to defend such a criminal. That didn't seem just at all!

As I might have implied earlier, I have a bit of a control issue. One day, as another new trial date loomed and I was praying and pleading with God for justice to be done within the legal system, I realized that I was praying down here on earth. How much more effective would Rebekah's prayers be while she was in heaven, right in the presence of God Himself! So I said to the Lord, "Lord, would you please tell Rebekah to pray for justice to be done?"

Poor Rebekah! Even when in heaven, her mother was still trying to tell her what to do.

I heard ever so clearly the Holy Spirit within me say, "Nancy Jo, Rebekah is perfectly happy and content to see justice done in My time and in My way. What's most important is that you are a good witness for Me."

I cannot express how freeing this truth was for me. I no longer placed my hope in justice being done by a broken justice system, a human judge, and a jury made up of twelve human beings. My hope in justice being done was transferred to my heavenly Father, who is *perfectly* just and never, ever fails His children—not me and not Rebekah.

Instead of reflecting little Davy's anxiety, fear, and irritation with those who saw things differently, I had Joseph's peace and confidence. God would take care of justice. He would take care of me and the trial and everyone involved, and He had already taken the very best care of Rebekah.

Did I still hope *for* justice? Absolutely! Did I still prepare an address to the jury explaining why my daughter's murderer should be punished to the full extent of the law? I most certainly did. Did I want him to be sentenced to prison? Yes! But no longer was my hope *in* any of these things happening. I genuinely cannot explain the burden that was lifted off of me that day.

Fifteen years later, I was reminded once again of my need to place my desire for justice in God's hands as we approached Ridge Huffman's parole hearing on January 28, 2024. Once again, David and I worked on our statements to the parole board, asking that he not be released. I relived a lot of the trauma of the murder itself as well as the stress of preparing to go to trial.

It made the fifteenth anniversary of Rebekah's murder extremely difficult in a whole new way. But I entered into the preparation knowing this: I was going to be OK either way! God would see justice done. God alone knew what was truly best for Ridge (his heart and his future), and God was the only One who had a true picture of what the outcome of "parole granted"/ "parole denied" would be.

I was still nervous! We did see some rules being bent in Ridge's favor, and that was hard. But I also had a peace and a confidence that God would once again work all things together for our good.

Parole was denied. I was and still am glad. I believe this was the right decision, especially when it was revealed that Ridge had not been following the rules of the prison. Yes, I would have been disappointed if parole had been granted. But I would not have despaired. Because my hope was not in the outcome of that hearing, it was in God!

How about a more common issue that more of us can relate to?

My husband, David, is a type 2 diabetic, and he likes to eat. He likes to eat pasta and bread and sweets! When my hope for his health rests in his doing the right things . . . well, can I just say that it does not bode well for our marriage?

For some reason, David does not welcome my policing of what he puts in his mouth. Strangely enough (insert sarcasm here), he isn't really interested in all the articles I read about things like diet Mountain Dew and artificial sweeteners and the perils therein. He doesn't even want to hear what my friend recently told me about diabetes, weight, exercise, supplements, and so on. Does that surprise you as much as it does me? I just don't get it, but this is the way it is!

When my hope is in David eating this or that, or taking a supplement, or exercising, or being thankful for all my research and input and profound wisdom, this is where I find myself: in a place of irritation, aggravation, and fear. *Hmmm* . . . sound familiar? I begin to think about how we will manage life with dialysis and become anxious, contemplating how I will cope financially if he dies.

Am I being melodramatic, or can you relate? Are you able to think of things besides God that you tend to place your hope in? A job, a relationship, a medication or doctor, a certain outcome. . . The list is endless.

To clarify once more: We can and we should hope *for* many things. There is nothing wrong with hoping for a good health report or a better job. In fact, there would be something wrong if we did *not* hope for things! Hope is a sustaining force in our lives.

The point is that as we hope for things, our hope needs to be anchored *in* God. Even then, hope can be elusive and difficult to hold on to during tumultuous times.

But how do we maintain hope in God when the things we hope for are stripped away or never materialize at all in the first place? When healing doesn't come. When the pregnancy strip never turns blue. When the job offer is never given. When those we love don't love us back. When we are living through a hell of our own making. When we are in a place of simply surviving one day at a time. When the permanency of death rips our world apart. *How?*

Chapter 2
Hope Anchored in Trust

When I was three years old, my parents and I lived in Bamberg, Germany, while my father was in military training. We eventually would move to the military base, but we first rented the top-floor apartment of a wonderful German family's home. It was tiny but conveniently located near the base and the little town where my mom and I could walk to do any necessary shopping.

There was a balcony off the living area that looked over the rolling countryside, and while it was indeed the second story, the way the house was positioned on a hill, the distance from the balcony to the ground was closer to two stories than one. The balcony itself was a simple slab of concrete with no railing or barrier whatsoever around it. Needless to say, I was not allowed outside unless it was with my mom or dad, and even then, I knew to stay safely up against the house and never go toward the edge.

One day, my mom took me out on the balcony as we waited for Daddy to come home from training. I was playing quietly in my safe little spot up against the house when I saw Daddy appear in the distance, walking toward home.

When he was right below the edge of the deck, knowing that I would never do so, he called out, "Nancy Jo! Jump to Daddy!" To both my parents' horror, I jumped up, ran straight to the edge of the concrete slab, and flung myself into the air.

Sixty years later, I'm alive and well, writing this book, so you know that my daddy caught me! Later, he would tell me how grateful he was that he had the sense to "give" with my body as he caught me. Although I was small, the long fall created a lot of momentum. At three years old, I had thought it was great fun and had no comprehension of what danger I was in.

But I assure you, the Lyttle house was not a happy one that evening. My mother was livid, and with good cause. Daddy said the only reason he called to me was because he *knew* I would not jump! Not when I had been taught to stay away from the edge, and most assuredly because I would be too afraid to jump from such a great height.

"Joe!" My mother countered. "You should have known she would jump! Nancy Jo will do anything you tell her to do!"

I want to encourage you to consider this true story from the perspective of how hope and trust are irrevocably linked. I had a certain "hope" that my daddy would catch me. More than that, really, because I didn't even stop to hope that he would catch me.

My trust in my father was so complete that I simply did what he told me to do. He had never failed to take care of me before. I knew he loved me. I knew I was safe with him. Can you see how the story would have played out differently if, in the past, my daddy had dropped me or done something that eroded my trust in him?

Perhaps you were not as blessed as I was to have had an earthly father in whom you could trust completely. Not that my father was perfect, as this story portrays! But I can say that I have never known a man of higher integrity and honor. I can also say that I never, ever questioned my daddy's love for me. It would have been impossible for a human being to love me better than he did until the day he died. And until the day Daddy died, I never had to hope he would be anything other than loving toward me. I never had any trouble trusting his word or trusting that he was acting in a way that he believed best for me.

I can imagine that might be hard to believe; after all, I was a teenager once. There were times I was extremely frustrated with him. We engaged in the kind of discussions most kids and parents do: "But, Daddy! Everybody else is doing it!"

His response to that was always the same: "Who is 'everybody'?"

Most of the time, I could only come up with a couple of names, and the point was moot. There was a time or two that I had a whole slew of names ready to recite. I would be eagerly anticipating victory, only for Daddy to respond to my impressive list with "Well, I'm not their daddy."

End of discussion. The thing is, although I certainly fussed at times, I knew I could trust my father to do what he thought was best for me.

When I was in high school, my dad came home from work one day with a deputy's badge. He told me that the sheriff's department had made him a deputy because of issues they were having at the Woodrow Wilson Rehabilitation Center, where he worked, and needed his help maintaining law and order.

Well, I thought that was really cool and proceeded to share this amazing honor with my friends at school . . . until one day at the dinner table, when Daddy said he had just been teasing me! Of course, I had to go tell all my friends that my dad wasn't really a deputy. But again, my trust in him was revealed.

My mom corrected me. "You need to learn to not believe everything people say!"

I replied, "*People* didn't tell me that—my daddy did!" And Daddy never lied. He was completely trustworthy and honest; he had just been playing with me.

In the same way, God has a wonderful sense of humor. But He never teases or tells us things that are not 100-percent accurate. His word is truth! If He says it, you can count on it. You can believe it with all your heart.

Take a look at Numbers 23:19:

> God is not a man, so He does not lie. He is not human, so He does not change His mind. Has He ever spoken and failed to act? Has he ever promised and not carried it through?

Now let's consider another illustration to solidify the correlation between trust and hope.

Picture a favorite chair in your home. Preferably a big, comfy, cushiony chair that you have had for a while. When you go to sit down, do you consciously think to yourself, "Boy, I sure do hope this chair doesn't collapse when I sit on it"? Of course not! You have "certain hope" that isn't even mentally processed because you trust that the chair will perform as it always has. You can plop yourself down without any worries.

Contrast this with going to the home of someone you don't know well. When you go into their living room, they gesture toward a rickety wooden chair. One of the cross rails is missing completely, another is hanging from one side, and the seat is a piece of woven fabric that you can see through in places. If you are adventurous enough to give it a shot, you will gently and gingerly sit down, consciously thinking that you sure do *hope* that chair doesn't collapse under you.

Aside from the visible reasons to have confidence in your personal chair versus the strange wooden chair, there are two more deciding factors to determine how much you entrust the chairs to hold you: First is your history with the chair itself. Your personal chair has never let you down in the past. Whereas the history of the other chair is completely unknown. Has *anyone* sat in it before—after it started to fall apart, that is?

Secondly, we specified that you did not know the person who offered the chair to you. This is key! If it were a trustworthy friend or family member—who, unlike Daddy, was not a jokester—you would likely trust them to care enough about your personal well-being to know that, appearance aside, the chair is trustworthy.

Now let's try to apply these truths—history with and how well we know another person—to our relationship with the Lord and how that relationship affects our trust, or our faith, in Him, which in turn, directly affects the strength of the hope we place in Him. We can't really rely on our eyes to be of much help in determining how worthy of trust the Lord is, but our knowledge of Him and our history (as well as the stories of others' history) with Him are key. In other words, the better our relationship with the Lord, the more we trust Him.

Chapter 3
Relationship That Builds Trust

I know some people quite well, and because I know them well, I know I cannot trust them. Why? There are many reasons: their past actions that directly affected me or others I know, their past choices that reveal character flaws or addictions or a lack of integrity, perhaps even a serious crime that was committed with no lasting sign of remorse or a desire to change.

The better you know a person, the better you can answer these kinds of questions: Do they keep their word? Do they respect you? Do they speak truthfully even when it might hurt? Do you trust that they genuinely want the best for you? Are they willing to sacrifice on your behalf (time, money, work, care, etc.)? Do you observe them being dependable and honest in other situations and with other people? Do they lash out at you or others in anger? Are their expectations of you fair and consistent? Do they come around when you are needy, sick, grieving, and suffering, or only when things are going well?

I'm guessing some names and faces came to mind as you read this, of both faithful, trustworthy friends and family, as well as those who are . . . not. Whichever category you placed those people in, you did so based on your history with them and how well or how long you have known them. Our relationship with the Lord is not much different. The same character traits that are revealed the better we know another person are the same character traits that help build our trust in the Lord.

As we spend time with Him (in His Word, in prayer, inviting Him into our everyday lives), we get to know Him better. The more years we spend with Him, the better we know Him (assuming we invest time with Him and follow Him closely during those years). As we get to know God's character—who He really is—and as we walk through various life situations with Him, our ability to trust Him grows. As our trust in Him and in His goodness grows, so does our hope, which is founded on God's goodness and His unwavering love for us.

Perhaps you need to take some time to sit and think—or even better, journal—about the times that the Lord has proven Himself faithful to you. Times of healing for yourself or a loved one. Times of provision: finances, a job, wisdom in what to do or say. Answered prayers. Protection in danger or on the road. Times when God worked a bad situation for your good. So often, we take God's work on our behalf for granted, either missing His hand entirely or attributing the work to ourselves, someone else, or maybe even luck.

James 1:17 tells us that every good gift comes down from God the Father. *Every* good gift! Romans 8:28 tells us that it is God who is working all things together for our good. One of the first steps in building your trust in the Lord is to recognize His loving, attentive care for you. We can see evidence of this easily in the good times and in the wonderfully answered prayers that we or others prayed on our behalf. But we can also find evidence in the bad times *if* we patiently look for it!

Having three children in three and a half years made for a very busy and tired Mommy! After Rebekah was born, I jokingly said that if I ever had anything hot to eat, I'd probably vomit it up because my stomach wouldn't know what to do with it! There was no sleeping in either. David worked long hours at UPS, and most of the time, when he got home, not only were the children in bed, but I was too . . . unless I was up feeding a baby, comforting someone after a bad dream, or nursing a sick child. Don't get me wrong: I would not trade those times for *anything*. But you can imagine how David and I might have longed for some time to ourselves.

I think Rebekah was about three when my parents graciously offered to start keeping the children at their house for a night or two so that David and I could have a little breather once a year. They would always come to Virginia in May for the Mid-Atlantic Wheelchair Games, which Daddy helped officiate. We would host them here for a few days, and then we would all head down in two vehicles to my parents' home in Georgia for David's annual two-week vacation. We would caravan to Duluth, which is a large subdivision outside of Atlanta. Daddy would treat us all to dinner, then the children would load up with their grandparents and go the rest of the way to Warm Springs, while David and I booked a hotel room there in Duluth. We would shop, eat out, see a movie, relax, and, most importantly, sleep in!

In May 1993, Rebekah was five; Joseph, seven; and Davy, eight. David and I were eagerly anticipating our alone time this year, and the children were excited for their time with Granddaddy and Mom-Mom.

All was going as planned until we started to go our separate ways in Duluth. It was dark as we all said our goodbyes in the restaurant's parking lot. Although they had been working perfectly the whole way to Duluth, Daddy's headlights would not come on when he started the car. Daddy had an important meeting the next morning and couldn't stay the night. It was late enough that no garages or auto parts stores were open.

There was only one option: David and I would lead the way to Warm Springs with Daddy following right behind us for the approximately forty-five-minute drive.

As we drove, David was not very happy with the Lord. (Haven't we all been there?) He was very disappointed (as was I) and saying things like, "Is two days away too much to ask, or too hard for God to pull off? Why couldn't God have let the lights work until they got home?"

I will never forget part of my response to his frustrated queries: "I don't think God sends angels around to pull the wires out of people's headlights so they don't work! I think you are blaming God when He didn't have anything to do with it."

We made it to my parents' safely, got the children tucked into bed, and planned to drive back to Duluth the next afternoon to start our special alone time a day later.

The next morning, I was awakened not by little ones but by the phone ringing. My grandfather, who had been receiving chemotherapy treatments for lung cancer, was having a hard time breathing and called to see if one of my parents could drive him to his doctor in Columbus. Knowing David would sleep in, I immediately offered to do so.

My father's parents were, to put it mildly, *difficult*. My grandmother, in particular, was very unkind. Well, to be brutally honest, she was cruel. My grandfather, I think, would have been a good man if it hadn't been for her influence. They were upstanding citizens, churchgoers, and had some good qualities, but they quite literally hated my mother. I think they only allowed enough love in their hearts for their son, and when he got married, they saw her as competition for his love and loyalty.

There is no need to go into all the dysfunction and unkindness my mother and I endured from my grandparents, but it is important to explain that as I grew older, I not only picked up more on their unkindness toward my mother and other loved ones, but I was also aware that my grandmother did not like me thinking for myself. My relationship with both of my grandparents grew strained. I did what was, unfortunately, my go-to response in difficult relationships: I withdrew. I avoided them. I am so sorry to say that while I was not disrespectful or rude, neither was I loving or even nice. My grandfather even asked my father why I didn't love them anymore at one point. So it was in the midst of this less-than-pleasant situation that I offered to drive them to the doctor.

What I had anticipated being a few hours turned into an all-day event. I drove my grandparents to the oncologist's office, where we learned that my grandfather had pneumonia, caused by the chemo. His doctor wanted to hospitalize him. I drove us straight to the hospital, and we went through the admission process.

Throughout the day, I was able to love on my grandfather, and my grandmother as well. Driving, chatting, pushing his wheelchair (which was necessary due to his severe shortness of breath), putting ointment on his very chapped lips, fetching him water, and so on. Nothing at all extraordinary, but throughout the day, I was able to convey to him that I genuinely cared for him, and he was so appreciative. I remember him saying they could not have paid a professional driver to have done a better job transporting him from place to place.

Late that afternoon, Daddy and David came to the hospital. While they were there, the doctor came into my grandfather's room and said that they had him on good antibiotics and expected him to respond well and be home in a day or two. I hugged my grandparents and Daddy goodbye and told my granddaddy that I loved him. Finally, David and I departed for Duluth, excited to be on our way!

I remember we ate dinner out. We may have shopped a little, but it was quite late by the time we had eaten and reserved our hotel room, so we may have just returned to the room and watched TV. I truly don't remember. What I do remember is being awakened at about 6:30 in the morning by a ringing telephone. It was Daddy, letting us know we needed to head back to their house; my grandfather had died very early that morning.

Two conversations from this time remain crystal clear all these years later. The first is the one I had with David on the way back to my parents' house. I told him that I had been mistaken before; God had indeed sent angels to mess with Daddy's headlights.

I am genuinely sorry that, in my immaturity, which went on for far too long, I failed to show love for my grandfather. I truly did love him, and I believe that he truly loved me. I will be forever grateful to God for giving me the most undeserved gift of having an entire day to serve and love on my granddaddy before he died, not only for his sake but also for mine. Had those headlights not malfunctioned, I would have never had the opportunity to express the genuine love that I had so childishly withheld from my grandfather for many years.

This leads to the second conversation that I remember so clearly:

I was in the bathroom at my parents' house, fixing my hair and makeup for the memorial service for my grandfather in Georgia. I spoke out loud to the Lord, asking Him to please help me remember His miraculous intervention for me whenever it seems something good has been taken from me or I feel like He does not care about me. I asked Him to help me specifically remember this when I cannot see His hand as clearly as I could see it in this situation, so that I would always trust in His loving-kindness, even when not understanding or seeing anything good.

Fifteen years later, as we walked through the aftermath of Rebekah's murder, I would remember this conversation with the Lord over and over again.

Perhaps you are reading this, appreciating that God came through for me but thinking that this has not been your experience. Or perhaps you are thinking I'm off my rocker to think God cares and is involved in our lives in an intimate way when my daughter was *murdered*. I'd like to address these two possible reactions, and I hope you will hang in here with me.

God hasn't been there for me. God has let me down. Have you ever had thoughts like these? I think there are two underlying reasons it can seem that God has abandoned us or failed to do what He has promised. The first is a very basic and prevalent misconception among Christians that is based upon false doctrine. Many churches/preachers teach that if we turn to Jesus, all things will be bright and rosy. Along the same vein, they teach that if only we will be obedient, if we are "good" Christians, then God owes us an easy life.

This teaching is vile and harmful! Most importantly, it is not found *anywhere* in Scripture. In fact, quite the opposite was stated by Jesus Himself: "I have told you all this so that you may have peace in me. Here on earth you will have many trials and sorrows. But take heart, because I have overcome the world" (John 16:33). Please note Jesus's words: "*many* trials *and* sorrows" (emphasis mine). Deciding to follow Jesus is not a free ticket to an easy life! If truth be told, that decision can make life here on earth in some ways much more difficult.

I am puzzled as to what exactly those who spread this teaching base it on. All the disciples, except for John, were martyred: crucified, stoned, beheaded, flayed alive. . . We have Paul's own testimony to what life held for him after his conversion: "Even now we go hungry and thirsty, and we don't have enough clothes to keep warm. We are often beaten and have no home" (1 Corinthians 4:11). And then this in 2 Corinthians 11:25–27:

> Three times I was beaten with rods. Once I was stoned. Three times I was shipwrecked. Once I spent a whole night and a day adrift at sea. I have traveled on many long journeys. I have faced danger from rivers and from robbers. I have faced danger from my own people, the Jews, as well as from the Gentiles. I have faced danger in the cities, in the deserts, and on the seas. And I have faced danger from men who claim to be believers but are not. I have worked hard and long, enduring many sleepless nights. I have been hungry and thirsty and have often gone without food. I have shivered in the cold, without enough clothing to keep me warm.

And we have Paul's reminder (Romans 8:35–39) that though

we will suffer, it does not mean we are not loved by Jesus:

> Can anything ever separate us from Christ's love? Does it mean he no longer loves us if we have trouble or calamity, or are persecuted, or hungry, or destitute, or in danger, or threatened with death? (As the Scriptures say, "For your sake we are killed every day; we are being slaughtered like sheep.") No, despite all these things, overwhelming victory is ours through Christ, who loved us.
>
> And I am convinced that nothing can ever separate us from God's love. Neither death nor life, neither angels nor demons, neither our fears for today nor our worries about tomorrow—not even the powers of hell can separate us from God's love. No power in the sky above or in the earth below—indeed, nothing in all creation will ever be able to separate us from the love of God that is revealed in Christ Jesus our Lord.

We also have James's admonishment in James 1:2–4:

> Dear brothers and sisters, when troubles of any kind come your way, consider it an opportunity for great joy. For you know that when your faith is tested, your endurance has a chance to grow. So let it grow, for when your endurance is fully developed, you will be perfect [mature] and complete, needing nothing.

When I worked on memorizing this passage, I would always emphasize it in a "well, duh!" kind of voice: "*Sooooo* let it grow!" I don't know about you, but when a trouble of any kind strikes, my first thoughts are usually not about letting anything positive grow but rather about God fixing whatever the trouble is and getting relief as quickly as possible! That confession aside, here we have another crystal-clear example from Scripture that troubles—and many different kinds of troubles—are part of life. We need to accept this fact of life and plan ahead of time how we are going to choose to respond to trouble.

I remember practicing an exercise to help me hear from the Lord. I pictured myself in a Bible story, talking to the Lord, then I wrote down what I saw, experienced, and heard from the Holy Spirit. I had been doing this and not hearing anything specific, until one day, when God spoke clearly to my heart.

Our family was in great turmoil and sadness several years after Rebekah's death. I was grieving over the situation and for each of the family members involved. And I was fearful of what the future held for us. So I chose my Bible story very carefully. I was in the midst of a terrible storm, and like anyone would, I wanted a happy ending! The Bible story I placed myself in was the one in which the disciples are caught in a storm on the water, fearing for their lives, while Jesus is sleeping in the bow of the boat. Upon awakening, Jesus immediately calms the storm (Mark 4:35–41).

I imagined myself in the boat, being tossed to and fro, holding on for dear life. Amid wind, waves, and flashes of lightning, I made my way to Jesus and woke Him up to explain the situation and my fears. I waited for Him to say, "Peace, be still! All will be well," and for the storm to die down. I will never forget what happened in my mind next.

Jesus did get up. He came with me to the edge of the boat and watched the raging storm. And then He placed His arm around me and guided me back to the middle of the boat to sit down. He held me close and said that the storm was going to carry on, but that He would be with me and with those I loved.

He was right. The storm did rage around us. And it was not fun. It was heartbreaking and left us with many deep wounds.

But He did walk through it with us! He did provide in wonderful ways. He did and continues to bring healing. And we pray and trust that the healing will continue.

We cannot put God in a box. We can't even put Him in a Bible story and force Him to write us a happy ending. But in the midst of storms, heartache, suffering, grief, injustice, disappointment, and more, we can trust Him to be with us and for us—working on our behalf and on behalf of those we love—even when we cannot see the results of His work.

God's will is never for tragedy, pain, sickness, grief, betrayal, or any other bad thing to befall us. Just look at Jesus: He cured the sick! Raised the dead! Set people free! Changed hearts and lives! And the Bible tells us that Jesus is the exact representation of God. He only did what He saw His Father doing.

Chapter 4
God's Will & God's Promises

You know the sayings "God is in control" and "God's will is always done"? Without being a nitpicker, I'd like to propose that we look at this concept again in a different light. If we see our life like a little remote-controlled car to which God holds the only controller, making the car go forward, turn, reverse, and stop at His will, then we have no other option than to hold God responsible when that little car runs into the furniture, over someone's toes, or into the road to be demolished by a real car!

I absolutely believe in the sovereignty of God. He is over all and in charge! This is the very reason He is able to work all things, even terrible things that are not His will for us, for our good and His glory. Hang in here with me, if this is causing you worry or skepticism.

Let's consider what Scripture says:

- If God's will is always done on earth, why did Jesus ask us to pray that it would be done in Matthew 6:10?
- Jesus tells us that Satan is the prince of this world in John 12:31 and 14:30.
- The devil has power! It is limited, but he does have au-

thority in this world that is only trumped by Jesus. We can walk in the authority of Christ, but not until heaven will we and those we love be free from the terrible influence and power of our great enemy, who is constantly prowling around like a lion looking for someone to devour (1 Peter 5:8).

I remember leading a GriefShare support group of some people who had experienced traumatic losses of children, siblings, and parents. They were struggling to trust a God who they perceived as having caused their loved ones to suffer and die, because, after all, it was "His will."

I finally asked them point-blank if they believed that God's will is always done here on earth. It was a unanimous "Yes!" My next question was "Do you ever sin?" Again, with nodding heads, the consensus was that, of course, they sin at times.

"Okay," I said, "so is it God's will that you sin?" I was met with utter silence. They were unable to process that question within the box that they had placed God and how He works in our world.

Because we live in a fallen world; because God does not revoke anyone's free will and people can steal, kill, drive drunk, abuse substances, and commit countless other wrongs; because our bodies are not impervious to disease, aging, mutations, and so on; because we have a hostile, active enemy who, although held on a leash, can inflict great harm and is literally hellbent on destroying the people God loves; because of all this, God's will is not always done here on earth. That is one of the reasons we long for heaven!

(As an aside: If _____ [death, pain, cancer, betrayal, etc.] is God's will, would that not mean it's in heaven too? Perish the thought! God's Word makes it clear that those things have no place there. Not only that, but we know from Scripture that death is an enemy that will be destroyed along with Satan.)

Because of these harsh realities of life on earth, some of the storms we wish to bypass us rage on. Some of the boxes we and, I believe, God would love to see filled (a happy marriage, good health, children who love and follow Jesus, provision, restoration of relationships, justice, and on and on) remain empty. If our hope is a pain-free life or a fulfilled wish, we are in trouble.

I have a friend who has been a second mom to me and a powerful prayer warrior. My friend loves God, serves God, and worships God alone. She is sold out for Jesus and has been for many, many years. Her husband is as well. As a young couple, Betty and Doug longed for children. They prayed as well as sought medical help for many years, but this precious box was never filled. When Betty's hope was in the box, when she felt like God was keeping something good—a baby—from her, she endured such terrible disappointment, heartache, anger, frustration, and desperation.

But there came a time when my friend transferred her hope to God: His character and His promises. She did it by answering and being obedient to God's call to surrender her box. Later, she would testify that God had been asking this of her for a long time. He was so kind, so patient, so loving during this time. She chose to set aside her box and to focus instead on God's love for her.

Betty found peace and joy in knowing that God loved her. Her infertility was not a judgment by Him, not a punishment from

Him. It broke His heart as it broke hers. But because God is God and His promises never fail, because Betty transferred her hope to God instead of the box, because she chose not to become bitter but to fully trust in God's promises and character, Betty has been filled with peace and joy. She has seen much good come from her heartache as she has allowed God to use it to make her more like Jesus.

Betty is a woman of God: full of love and grace and a tremendous encourager, who has more "children" and "grandchildren" than you could shake a stick at! Now, I do not mean to say that the moment she chose to place her hope in God alone, she stopped grieving. She still gets slammed by grief. It's not that she wouldn't love to go back and change the plot, writing in a child of her and Doug's own. But even in the grief, there is joy and peace because the God of hope fills her with these qualities of Himself as she continues to place her trust and hope in Him.

The truth is that life is hard! Life includes pain, sorrow, tragedy, and grief. It is full of injustice and unfairness and great suffering, whether we believe in Jesus or not. The choice is this: *Do I go through life, which will be terribly difficult at times, with or without Jesus?*

I choose *with*! If we can step away from the ludicrous, false teaching that God "owes" us anything at all and simply be filled with gratitude for His faithfulness, forgiveness, mercy, and grace, among a multitude of other things, we won't be caught off guard when life in a fallen world throws us a curveball.

Perhaps you never thought life would be perfect but believe God failed to keep His promise to you at some point in time — in some desperate situation that you or a loved one faced.

This past year, we had major flooding in our area. Here is a journal entry from October 6, 2024, which I posted on Facebook:

> Today, as we sang "Way Maker" in church and proclaimed God as "promise keeper," I was reminded of a conversation I had with Joanna recently. [Joanna is my seven-year-old granddaughter.]
>
> Joseph and his family had come to stay with us because they lost power as Helene surged through our area. Joanna and I were in the living room while she played and I worked on my to-do list or something. I can't remember what was said to precipitate her comment, but she stated as the rain poured and the winds blew, "Well, at least we know it won't flood!"
>
> I said, "Joanna, honey, it *is* flooding."
>
> With eyes wide and in a hurtful, surprised tone, she cried out, "Then God didn't keep His promise!"
>
> I explained that God did not say there would never be any more floods! He said He would never send a flood to cover the whole earth again. Joanna accepted this with relief and went back to playing.
>
> This morning, as we sang of our good, good God who makes ways, keeps promises, and lights up the darkness, I found myself wondering how often we adults accuse God of not keeping His promises, when in reality, He never made any such promise or how often we have misinterpreted/misapplied a promise He did make.
>
> For example, "God will never give you more than you can handle."[2] This very common statement is found nowhere in Scrip-

---

2. This common quip is based upon Scripture that is taken out of context, misapplied, and then, from this inaccurate position, misquot-

ture! It assumes everything that comes our way (specifically the bad) is from God. That in itself is completely false. What about 2 Corinthians 1:8 (ESV), where Paul says, "For we were so utterly burdened beyond our strength that we despaired of life itself"?

We all will most likely face things in this life that are way beyond our ability to handle. I certainly have! That's why (one of the multitude of reasons why!) I need Jesus. He is my Strength, my Help, my Refuge, the Lifter of my Head, when life bombards me with things I most assuredly cannot handle on my own.

What about that generic promise (maybe *assumption* is a better word) that if we follow Jesus, all will be well? Not only is this not a promise, but it is in direct contradiction of what Jesus Himself told us: "In this world you will have troubles" (John 16:33 NIV). Jesus tells us not to lose hope, for He has overcome the world, yes! But that does not negate the fact that we *will* have troubles, and many of them.

What about these common "misunderstandings"? If we just pray and believe, none of our loved ones will suffer or die, and we ourselves can live in perfect health. I can ask for anything and just tack on "in Jesus' name," and I'll get it! That if I pray, literal storms will bypass my home. That if I'm sick and not healed, it must be because of sin in my life or because my faith isn't strong enough. People may not come out and state these things in such explicit words (although they sometimes do), but the implication is there.

---

ed. First Corinthians 10:13 says, "The temptations in your life are no different from what others experience. And God is faithful. He will not allow the temptation to be more than you can stand. When you are tempted, he will show you a way out so that you can endure." It is clear that Paul is not speaking of trials, tribulations, or anything other than *temptations*. And to take it a step further, even here, it is God who provides and shows the way to resist, endure, and come out victorious on the other side.

These are misinterpreted/misapplied scriptures. Yes: God still heals and even raises the dead! He transforms hearts and lives! He still miraculously intervenes in our lives and in this world! And He can and has redirected storms! But He does so as He knows best, *not* at our command or demand. A failure to be healed or to see a loved one healed or not receiving something we ask for in prayer is not evidence of God not keeping a promise. It *is* evidence of the fact that we live in a fallen world where Satan has great power, life is not fair, justice is not done, and the earth is groaning as in the pains of childbirth (1 John 5:19, Romans 8:22). It is also, at times, evidence that God knows better than we do what is best for us and those we love. *And* it can also be evidence that God does not force anyone to do anything!

There are lots of promises of God we can stand on. They will never fail because God is unable to not keep His promises! He is always faithful. Always! When it seems He isn't, it's because we look through a glass darkly. It's because we only see what is temporal, what is visible to the human eye. This is when we choose: *Do I believe God or not?* I can say, "I do not understand." "I do not like it." "Oh, how I wish things were different!" But in spite of my circumstances, in the face of unanswered prayers (or those not answered in the way I want them to be), I can trust the God who made me and who loves me to keep His promises. And to one day reveal to me just how He did so, even in the most devastating and traumatic times.

This promise is my favorite (or at least one of my *top* favorites)! This promise is always true for those who have surrendered to Jesus: "And we *know* that God causes *all things* to work together for good to those who love God, to those who are called according to His purpose" (Romans 8:28 NASB, emphasis mine).

All things! Even hard and horrible things that are not caused by God can be *used* by God to change me into the image of Jesus.

God *always* keeps His promises. He is the Promise Keeper, after all!

I touched on this in my Facebook post, but let me explain my reasoning in stating that God never fails to keep His promises while still grieving the loss of my daughter, Rebekah.

This world is certainly not the paradise that God originally created. People have free will. Laws are imperfect, and our justice system is broken. (At least we have a justice system, but it is indeed flawed.) We suffer the consequences of our sins, and unfortunately, we suffer the consequences of other people's sins. We live in a fallen world, and Satan is its ruler.

God is the giver of every good and perfect gift (James 1:17). Cancer, murder, injustice, hunger, abuse, sex trafficking, addiction . . . none of these are good gifts, and the list is endless. God does *not* give us these things. They are simply a result of living where God's will is not always done—no matter how hard we pray.

The first bit of good news is that this is not all there is! Heaven is coming, and it will be that perfect, wonderful, no-sorrow, no-pain, "heavenly" forever-life that we all instinctively long for. Second, as stated in Romans 8:28 above, God will work for our good during whatever circumstances we find ourselves. And third, we don't have to walk through the agony of life here on earth alone. Jesus desires to walk it with us.

I'm sure there is more good news I could share, but I'm trusting—I'm *hoping*—you get my point!

Chapter 5
Trust Him

You may be asking, "How do I build my trust in God?" I'll tell you how you can start right now. First, go back and look for His hand in your past and in the pasts of those you love. Once you start looking, you will surely find evidence of God's goodness and intervention in your life.

Next, choose to either trust Him for the first time or to work on building the trust you already have in Him. Practically, this process can look different for each of us. For all of us, it means to place everything in His hands: ourselves, others, and our situations. It absolutely includes prayer and the conscious choice to say, "Lord, I trust You with _____."

I highly encourage you to look for biblical promises that apply to you today, being careful to take them in context. Romans 8:28 is a great place to start, along with Deuteronomy 31:8 (NIV): "The LORD himself goes before you and will be with you; he will never leave you nor forsake you. Do not be afraid; do not be discouraged."

I also love John 5:17—"My Father is always working and so am I"—when it seems like God isn't hearing my prayers. But I think my favorite is Hebrews 10:23: "Let us hold tightly without wavering to the hope we affirm, for God can be trusted to keep his promise."

(For more, see the collection of my favorite Scriptures in the back of the book.)

I have sought to help you understand the link between hope and trust in God. But this is not my original idea. Check out Romans 15:13 (emphasis mine):

> I pray that God, the *source of hope*, will fill you completely with joy and peace *because* you trust in Him. *Then* you will overflow with confident hope through the power of the Holy Spirit.

Trust is imperative, dear friend. And because it is a command from God that we trust Him, He will indeed help us build our trust in Him. Don't ever be afraid to jump into the arms of your never-failing, ever-faithful God. It is literally impossible for Him to be untrustworthy or unfaithful.

"If we have no faith, He will still be faithful for He cannot go against what He is" (2 Timothy 2:13 NLV).

So here we are! We have defined *hope*. We understand the difference between hoping for something and hoping in something, the latter preferably being God. And we understand that it is hard to hope in anyone or anything that we do not trust. We've even touched on how to build our trust in God.

Now, we are ready to look at this hope we have in depth.

II.
TRUTHS

Chapter 6
God Goes Before Us

I have an outline that I return to again and again to encourage myself and those I speak to. It's not because I can't think of anything new—I am constantly revising it with new examples—but because it is so very profound to me. I find myself perpetually turning to these three main truths to crush fear, to deal with disappointments and concerns, to rein in my wandering thoughts, and to find freedom from the crushing grief of loss and regret over my own failures. These simple truths, based on Psalm 139 and Deuteronomy 31:8, are the building blocks for the hope that can lift us out of our past, carry us through our present, and give us promise for the future.

The first is that God always goes before us. There are so many ways God has done this in my life. I could probably write an entire book just about them! And these are only the ways I know and have seen Him go before me. I'm sure there are a multitude of other instances that I am completely unaware of! However, never in my life has God going before me been as evident as it was the day Rebekah was murdered. Not only that, but I cannot imagine ever being more grateful for Him going before me.

"Joseph never, *ever* answered the phone," I began my first book, *Safe in Your Arms*, which is about Rebekah's murder. But on the morning of January 28, 2009, my twenty-two-year-old son, Joseph, chose not to go to class because of snow and answered the phone call that would change our lives forever. Here's another excerpt from that book:

> On the other end of that phone call, which Joseph had inexplicably answered that late January morning, was Ridge's brother with the news that Ridge had murdered Rebekah. Like I said before, Joseph never answered the phone, and yet this day, he did. This intervention could have only been the grace and mercy of God.
>
> Joseph, most certainly led and empowered by the Holy Spirit, hung up and dialed the Buckhannon Police Department to verify what he had been told. Once the police confirmed that Ridge had murdered his sister, Joseph began making other phone calls: to his dad, who was mercifully close to the UPS headquarters; to his brother, Davy, and his wife, Jennifer; to our friends Henry and Virginia Wingfield; to David's and my sisters; among others.
>
> I am still in awe of this young man and the precise, mature, and wise decisions he made that day. His incredible inner strength and love for me enabled him to shield me until I was surrounded by those who loved me.

That was definitely one of the more dramatic mercies I've experienced. Let me share a more recent story, which may pale in comparison but shows how God cares about even small issues in our lives.

A few years ago, our dishwasher broke. It was only about three years old, so we were hopeful that it would be an easy fix. David called a repairman, who was not only very kind but also very honest. After checking out the dishwasher, he explained all the details to David in the kitchen, while I sat in the living room within easy earshot. The electrical control panel, for whatever reason, had quit working.

To make a technical conversation simple, we had two choices: We could pay to fix the dishwasher's electrical panel, which would cost us about five to six hundred dollars, or we could purchase a new dishwasher. David asked the repairman what he would do if it were his dishwasher, and he said he would replace it. Then they discussed what brand to purchase so we wouldn't end up in the same boat in three more years! He provided several name brands along with their approximate costs. We would be looking at close to one thousand dollars to get a solid dishwasher—one that would clean well and endure.

While this conversation was happening, I was planning how to convince David not to replace the dishwasher. I had gone through seasons without one before, and I was perfectly capable of doing so again. Sure, a dishwasher is handy. I have always been grateful when I did have one, but I did not *need* one!

I honestly cannot remember what bills or other costs were hanging over our heads at the time, but I had my arsenal of all the more important things than a new dishwasher all ready and lined up for when the repairman left.

But David was not moved by my list.

My husband has always been a hard worker. At one point, while he was working full time at UPS, he would also work at a friend's business, as time allowed. On weekends, he cleaned up fallen trees, some of which became firewood for our woodstove and some of which we sold and he delivered for an extra source of income.

Unable to help with ordinary household chores, David did not clean, cook, do laundry, or anything along those lines. But he has *always* reliably provided me with the best "help" he could by insisting on purchasing the best appliances we could afford. And for the most part, they have proved to be well worth the bit of extra money invested because of their performance and longevity. This time was not an exception to his desire to take care of me. But I was remaining firm! And he really couldn't argue against my list of our other priorities. He was just adamantly placing my needs first.

When we reached a stalemate in this lively conversation, I went out to get the mail. (I'm shaking my head as I write this.) In the mailbox was a sweet note from a dear friend that I had not seen in well over a decade. She lives out of state, and while she has kept in touch with my mom, I had not seen or communicated with her in all that time.

In her note, she wrote that the Lord had placed me on her heart, told her to send me the enclosed check, and told her that I would know what it was for. Want to hazard a guess at the amount of the check that I received out of the blue from a friend I hadn't seen or talked to for years?

"The Lord laid on my heart," she wrote, "to send $1,000 to you. Even though I don't know the reason behind it, I am delighted to obey and be the channel where you, a sister in the Lord, would feel the Father's love."

I just can't get over God's goodness and this precious friend's obedience!

I showed David the note and the check. He was amazed, but his eyes did not fill with tears as mine did. I think perhaps he was basking in God's affirmation of his point of view and trying to refrain from saying, "I told you so!"

I had no more arguments. Oh, God and His tender, extravagant care! I am still, to this day, blown away. Not only because of His love and concern over something as eternally trivial as a dishwasher, but I am also in awe of His timing. Had that check arrived any earlier, it would have been spent on one of those other important things on my list. Not wasted, but nonetheless, no longer available to purchase a dishwasher. Had it arrived even a day later, it would not have been so crystal clear as to which item on my list of needs was most important or if I should get the new dishwasher. I've jokingly (but at the same time seriously) said that if God can get the United States Post Office to deliver a letter on the exact day and to the exact hour it needed to be delivered, He really can do anything!

Just to put the icing on top, would you care to fathom a guess as to how much the new, beloved, best-we've-ever-had dishwasher cost?

David did a lot of research and found one that he genuinely thought was the best. We found it at a local, family-run store that we frequent whenever possible for a few hundred over the thousand dollars we had. I really liked it but did not want to spend the extra money.

We came home, and David got on the computer while I started cooking. He asked me how long until dinner was ready. I told him, and he said we had to eat and then run. Another local store had the exact same dishwasher on sale, but the sale ended . . . wait for it . . . that very evening!

We purchased the dishwasher, delivery, and a three-year protection plan (we usually do not opt in on those), and the total was just *under* a thousand dollars. A dear family member installed it for us for free.

I don't think I've ever had an appliance that I have been more grateful for, nor one that I have verbally thanked the Lord for more often! About a year later, I had major surgery, and I'm certain you can imagine what a blessing it was to have a dishwasher. And there have been a multitude of times when I have not only been thankful but thought, "Aha! Here's another reason the Lord wanted me to have this dishwasher!"

Big things, little things, life-altering, horrendous things . . . God goes before us into each and every situation. He knows us and He sets in motion things that are out of our control, even out of our imaginings, to meet the needs of His beloved children, to tenderly, lovingly care for us—body, mind, soul, and spirit.

I have hope because I *know* that no matter what this afternoon or tomorrow or next week or next year or the next ten years bring, God has lovingly gone before me and is already there, working on my behalf for what He alone knows I'll need.

Because of this, I can remain in the present, not wasting time being fearful over the future.

Chapter 7
God Walks With Us

Isaiah 43:1–3:

> But now, O Jacob, listen to the Lord who created you. O Israel, the one who formed you says, "Do not be afraid, for I have ransomed you. I have called you by name; you are mine. When you go through deep waters, I will be with you. When you go through rivers of difficulty, you will not drown. When you walk through the fire of oppression, you will not be burned up; the flames will not consume you. For I am the Lord, your God, the Holy One of Israel, your Savior."

Again, it is clear that our loving God does not exempt us from trials or troubles. But His Word assures us that we will not face those things alone.

I love the story of Shadrach, Meshach, and Abednego, found in the book of Daniel. These three brave men had been taken captive as young teens and removed from their homeland, forced to serve in an enemy king's land. Even the names we know them by were not their original names.

There came a day when these three were faced with a crucial

choice: Bow down before a statue of the king and disobey God's command not to worship other gods or be thrown into a furnace of blazing fire and die. This is a pretty good example of a life-or-death decision! But for these three who had experienced God's faithfulness and protection before, there really was no choice. They would obey God no matter the consequences.

So they did not bow. Three lone men among a multitude, they stuck out like a sore thumb. And they were reported to the king, Nebuchadnezzar, who had made the decree that anyone who did not bow to the idol he had ordered made in his image would be killed immediately.

Daniel 3:13–15:

> Then Nebuchadnezzar flew into a rage and ordered that Shadrach, Meshach, and Abednego be brought before him. When they were brought in, Nebuchadnezzar said to them, "Is it true, Shadrach, Meshach, and Abednego, that you refuse to serve my gods or to worship the gold statue I have set up? I will give you one more chance to bow down and worship the statue I have made when you hear the sound of the musical instruments. But if you refuse, you will be thrown immediately into the blazing furnace. And then what god will be able to rescue you from my power?"

I have always found it interesting that the king was willing to give these three a second chance. I believe it was because they had served him well up to this point. They were valuable to him. I think this is to show us that we can work for ungodly people; we can be under the authority of ungodly leadership in our state and nation, and we can choose to obey the powers that be and serve them well . . . *until* they demand something of us that contradicts God's specific commands. At that point, we too have a choice. May God give us the courage to always choose Him—no matter the consequences.

Daniel 3:16–18:

> Shadrach, Meshach, and Abednego replied, "O Nebuchadnezzar, we do not need to defend ourselves before you. If we are thrown into the blazing furnace, the God whom we serve is able to save us. He will rescue us from your power, Your Majesty. But even if he doesn't, we want to make it clear to you, Your Majesty, that we will never serve your gods or worship the gold statue you have set up."

Look carefully at the words they spoke to the ruling authority of the land. Do you recognize the respect they gave the king? They both honored his earthly position and authority over them while simultaneously making it clear that there was One who had even greater authority over them and their lives than King Nebuchadnezzar and that this was the One they would be obeying!

I love the testimony they gave to the king: *We serve a God who is able to save! He will rescue us! But even if he doesn't . . . we will never serve or worship another god.*

Let's examine their message, which may sound contradictory:

- God is able to save.
- God will rescue us.
- But even if he doesn't—

Wait. What? I thought they boldly told the king that God would rescue them.

This is how I understand their words and apply them to my life.

God is able: Our God is a mighty, miracle-working, mountain-moving, healer, deliverer, and death-defeating God!

God will rescue us: Our eternity is secure because God is our God. He secured our eternal future in Christ Jesus's work on the cross because we have accepted Christ as our Savior and Lord and have chosen to follow Him.

But even if He doesn't: God might miraculously save us from this trial. (God might heal us or our loved ones. God might calm the storm in an instant. God *might*. . .) But even if He does not intervene immediately or in a way we can discern here on earth, God alone is our God, and He will never allow you or anyone or anything else to usurp His position of leadership in our lives. Even if God does not answer our prayers the way we want Him to (even if we suffer, even if we grieve, even if all manner of difficulties and hardships are part of our life here on earth), God alone is our God, and we will obey Him no matter the cost. We will believe and trust in Him alone!

Daniel 3:19–23:

> Nebuchadnezzar was so furious with Shadrach, Meshach, and Abednego that his face became distorted with rage. He commanded that the furnace be heated seven times hotter than usual. Then he ordered some of the strongest men of his army to bind Shadrach, Meshach, and Abednego and throw them into the blazing furnace. So they tied them up and threw them into the furnace, fully dressed in their pants, turbans, robes, and other garments. And because the king, in his anger, had demanded such a hot fire in the furnace, the flames killed the soldiers as they threw the three men in. So Shadrach, Meshach, and Abednego, securely tied, fell into the roaring flames.

And with that, Nebuchadnezzar's true self is revealed. The

world has a way of making ugly things pretty. Hiding them behind gold and silver, power, flattery, and position. But take a stand against them, and the wrappings are stripped away. Nebuchadnezzar, who had benefited from the service of these three men, transformed from a gracious giver of second chances to an enraged, crazed tyrant, so focused on destroying them that he did not even care for the safety of his other obedient servants.

What do you think were the thoughts going through Shadrach's, Meshach's, and Abednego's minds as they were tied up, led to the furnace, and sent toppling into the raging flames? "Well, at least we obeyed God." "I really didn't think it would end this way!" "O God, are you there?" "God, I am afraid!" "God, I don't want to burn alive!" "God, help me!" Perhaps every step of the way, they expected an angel to deliver them or for Nebuchadnezzar to change his mind or die on the spot or . . . *something*. Anything to keep them from this horrible ending.

Have you been there? I have! Wanting God to do anything that would keep me (or one I love) from suffering.

But God seemed not to show up. Nothing happened to save them from being immersed in a scorching furnace of fire.

Daniel 3:24–27:

> But suddenly, Nebuchadnezzar jumped up in amazement and exclaimed to his advisers, "Didn't we tie up three men and throw them into the furnace?"
>
> "Yes, Your Majesty, we certainly did," they replied.
>
> "Look!" Nebuchadnezzar shouted. "I see four men, unbound,

walking around in the fire unharmed! And the fourth looks like a god!"

Then Nebuchadnezzar came as close as he could to the door of the flaming furnace and shouted: "Shadrach, Meshach, and Abednego, servants of the Most High God, come out! Come here!"

So Shadrach, Meshach, and Abednego stepped out of the fire. Then the high officers, officials, governors, and advisers crowded around them and saw that the fire had not touched them. Not a hair on their heads was singed, and their clothing was not scorched. They didn't even smell of smoke!

Oh, how we would love for life to truly be a "bed of roses"! How our hearts long for happy endings to every chapter of our lives, like in the books we read and the movies we watch. Might I say that there is a good reason for this longing?

One that is not utterly based in selfishness but rather based in biblical truth: God did not create us for suffering. God did not create us to die. God did not create us to grieve. All this is outside of His perfect will for us, His treasured creation! So when we are immersed in such things that are outside of God's original plan, these thoughts and feelings of "It shouldn't be this way!" are valid.

But as we read in Isaiah 43, deep waters, rivers of difficulty, and painful, destructive fires are part of living in our temporal world. However, as Shadrach, Meshach, and Abednego's story reveals, we do not travel through these devastating times alone.

Just as Jesus was right there with them in the furnace, so is He with us in our furnaces. Just as He walked with those three men through the fire, so He walks with *us*. Just as He unbound them, so He can work to set us free from that which has bound us for years. And just as He protected them from what would have killed them, He can protect us from the things that would destroy our hearts, minds, spirits, and bodies. And He will protect us from anything that would destroy our eternal souls.

Daniel 3:28–30:

> Then Nebuchadnezzar said, "Praise to the God of Shadrach, Meshach, and Abednego! He sent his angel to rescue his servants who trusted in him. They defied the king's command and were willing to die rather than serve or worship any god except their own God. Therefore, I make this decree: If any people, whatever their race or nation or language, speak a word against the God of Shadrach, Meshach, and Abednego, they will be torn limb from limb, and their houses will be turned into heaps of rubble. There is no other god who can rescue like this!"
>
> Then the king promoted Shadrach, Meshach, and Abednego to even higher positions in the province of Babylon.

Like Shadrach, Meshach, and Abednego, we will have a testimony of God's power, grace, provision, mercy, and love that will prayerfully point others to Him and encourage those who are in their own fiery furnace. This is the motivation behind this little book—behind every "sermon" I have shared, every talk I have given. To give others a glimpse of the incredible faithfulness of God in my own personal fiery furnace. My prayer and deep desire is that others will recognize God's hand in their own lives. That they would know He is indeed a good, good Father, and that He is for us and *utterly* trustworthy. And that those who hear or read my story will put their hope and trust in Him alone.

Chapter 8
God Follows After Us

We know that God goes before us. As only He can. This truly blows my mind! And God walks with us. It is the only way we can survive and even thrive during the difficulties life throws our way. It is the only way we can have hope in the pits in which we find ourselves.

But did you know that God follows behind you, redeeming your past?

Oh, the hope that gives me personally! I cannot imagine the unbearable grief of believing that all my past sins, failures, mistakes, poor choices, and even the past injustices, betrayals, and cruelties of others have no purpose and cannot be redeemed.

Let's look at some different definitions for the word *redeem* and see how the truth that "God works all things together for our good" can give us hope!

To redeem means
- to atone for (redeem an error).
- to offset the bad effect of.
- to free from what distresses or harms.

- to extricate from or help to overcome something detrimental.
- to change for the better.

This is what helps us stay in the present, dear ones, even after great failures, horrific injustices, brutal pain, and so on. We can place our past in God's hands, knowing He will redeem all things and work all things for *our* good—even things that are not His will.

Consider Joseph of the Old Testament. He was sold by his brothers into slavery in Egypt. There, he worked as a slave in the house of a man named Potiphar, was falsely accused by Potiphar's wife of trying to rape her (when in reality, he was refusing *her* sexual advances), and was thrown into prison. While in prison, he successfully interpreted the dreams of two of Pharaoh's officials who were also imprisoned. Although one was released and reinstated, just as Joseph said he would be, it wasn't until two years later, when Pharaoh needed a dream interpreted, that the cupbearer would mention the talent of the young Hebrew he had met in prison.

My study Bible says that it was thirteen years between the time that Joseph was sold into slavery and when he was released from prison and placed in charge of Pharaoh's palace. Only the pharaoh was greater in the hierarchy of Egyptian leadership. Even then, Joseph was still in a foreign country, serving under a pagan ruler, and separated from his family and all he knew and loved.

Many years after being elevated to this position of leadership, Joseph was reunited with his brothers. They were the same ones who betrayed him, treated him cruelly, cost him his relationship with his father and little brother, and instigated the entire years-long nightmare. This is what he said to them

(Genesis 45:4–8):

> I am Joseph, your brother, whom you sold into slavery in Egypt. But don't be upset, and don't be angry with yourselves for selling me to this place. It was God who sent me here ahead of you to preserve your lives. . . God has sent me ahead of you to keep you and your families alive and to preserve many survivors. So it was God who sent me here, not you! And he is the one who made me an adviser to Pharaoh—the manager of his entire palace and the governor of all Egypt.

Then years later, after his father's death, Joseph reassured them (Genesis 50:19–20, emphasis mine): "Don't be afraid of me. Am I God, that I can punish you? *You intended to harm me, but God intended it all for good.*"

Can you see the redemption God worked? He "offset the bad effect(s) of" Joseph's brothers' betrayal, Potiphar's wife's false accusations, and the cupbearer's forgetfulness! God set Joseph free from slavery, elevating him to a place of immense power. And God changed Joseph for the better. Joseph became a man of humility, quick to forgive rather than boasting about his dreams of being greater than his brothers.

I love the story of Joseph! It's important to remember that Joseph was a real person. While we can read his entire story and be filled with encouragement in a matter of minutes, Joseph endured thirteen years of slavery and prison. Thirteen years in the pit, during which he continued to believe in and be obedient to God. Imagine the humiliation of false accusations, the dark, dank confines of prison, a pit that was deep and seemingly never-ending. Joseph was a man of God, but he was also human. I'm sure he cried out at times about the injustice and wondered where God was. But he never turned his back on God. He continued to believe in, follow, and obey God.

And guess what... God was with Joseph in Egypt! While in Potiphar's house, we are told, "The LORD was with Joseph, so he succeeded in everything he did as he served in the home of his Egyptian master. Potiphar noticed this and realized that the LORD was with Joseph" (Genesis 39:2–3).

> But the LORD was with Joseph in the prison and showed him His faithful love. And the LORD made Joseph a favorite with the prison warden. Before long, the warden put Joseph in charge of all the other prisoners and over everything that happened in the prison. The warden had no more worries, because Joseph took care of everything. The LORD was with him and caused everything he did to succeed (Genesis 39:21–23).

This story takes us full circle in our understanding of God going before us, walking with us, and following behind us to redeem. And it is so important that we recognize our part in this redemption process! God worked—God worked miraculously—*but* God had a willing participant. Joseph did not trap himself or his brothers in the prison of unforgiveness. Joseph did not submit to sexual temptation. Joseph did not have a thirteen-year-long pity party. In every single horrible situation, Joseph stayed faithful to the God he could not see, but who was with him, loving him faithfully.

Is this not the most encouraging, most wonderful part of our journey through storms? God is also with *us*. He is also loving us. He is also faithful to us. He is also working all things together for our good—*all* things! It is up to us, dear reader. Do we cooperate like Joseph? Do we walk in obedience so that all God's good plans for us are fulfilled? Do we live a life that is so marked by the hand of God that it reveals even to unbelievers that the Lord is with us—even if they do not understand that it is the one true God who has come through for us?

Of all the ways God has been with me through every storm, but especially after Rebekah's murder, I am most grateful for His redemption. To endure such a storm, to survive such a deep pit of despair, to live through what my husband, David, says we would not wish on our worst enemy and not be changed would be the greatest tragedy I can imagine.

As you read the coming chapters, you will learn that I am not the person I used to be. Oh, how grateful I am for that! (And David is too!) I am not yet who God created me to be. I still struggle and fail. But I am not who I was—praise God! The Lord has used my past, Rebekah's murder, and my grief to make me more like Jesus.

He has taken my grief and the lessons I learned and empowered me to comfort others. He has taken my failures and grief and love for Rebekah and empowered me to write a book—*two* books now!

I no longer have Rebekah here on earth to love, but God gives me opportunities to show love and pour out the grace that I withheld for so long. He allows me to receive His abundant, amazing grace, for which I failed to realize I was utterly desperate.

We are just getting started, and much more is to come. But if you receive any insight, any encouragement from what you read in this little book; if you learn anything you want to put into practice; if you close this book with more hope, or feel determined with God's help to build hope; if you have received anything at all good from what I have shared, it is God miraculously and beautifully redeeming my past.

He is no respecter of persons, and He will do the same for you! It will look different because you and I are different, as are our pasts. But those differences do not hinder His ability to follow behind and redeem.

It is God's ability to redeem that carries us forward in hope when everything we have hoped *for* does not come to pass.

Now that we know the truth that God goes before us, with us, and after us, let's go back to that darkest place, where we feel the most alone, the most helpless, and the most hopeless. But this time, don't be afraid, dear one. Our Hope is closer than you could ever imagine.

III.
TRAPPED

Chapter 9
In the Pit of Despair

Psalm 40:1–3 became my life verses after Rebekah's murder. The beginning of that passage says,

> I waited patiently for the LORD to help me
> and He turned to me and heard my cry.
> He lifted me out of the pit of despair,
> out of the mud and the mire,
> and set my feet on solid ground.

From the psalmist's perspective, at least as far as we can surmise from the first line, he was in the pit alone. God's back was turned to him. He wasn't hearing David's cries. God seemed absent in the pit of despair. David wallowed in the mud and mire alone. Hurting. Abandoned. Unseen. Unloved. Unable to see God's hand.

I believe we have all experienced this misperception at one time or lots. It is a huge part of what makes that pit of despair so inky dark, so crushing, so overwhelming, so hard to find hope within.

The reality is that if we have accepted Jesus as Savior and

Lord and decided to follow Him in obedience to His Word, then "God will never leave us or forsake us" (Deuteronomy 31:8, Hebrews 13:5). In spite of this unshakable truth that we cling to, it can sure seem like we are utterly alone and forsaken in that oppressive darkness.

I remember an illustration Paul David Tripp used in a GriefShare video. He described sitting in a dark basement in the middle of the day, with no lights and all windows covered with heavy drapes. Even when we are unable to see the sunshine, it does not change the reality that the sun is shining brilliantly in the sky. But in the basement, we are unable to see the light. That, he shared, is the way it is with grief. For a season, it blinds us to God's presence. It may hide other things, too, such as hope, joy, and peace.

We must cling to the truth that despite the dark, the cold, the muck, and the web of broken dreams, broken hearts, broken bodies, broken relationships—whatever our pit consists of— God *is* with us. He has gone before us and is waiting for us, preparing a place for us where there will never be any darkness, despair, suffering, or pain!

And right at the moment when we feel we cannot go on, right at the moment when we are tempted to give up or give in, right at the moment when things "can't get any worse" and yet somehow manage to spiral even further down, God is *still* with us. He is holding us and comforting us. He is as close as our breath. As a matter of fact, He is residing with*in* us! And His Holy Spirit is pleading for us when we cannot even find the energy, the words, or the know-how to plead for ourselves (Romans 8:26–27).

We cannot see God. We may not feel His presence. We may not hear His voice. But He is with us. And He is close to us.

Psalm 56:8:

> You keep track of all my sorrows.
> You have collected all my tears in your bottle.
> You have recorded each one in your book.

I knew this verse and always loved it, but when I read Psalm 38:9 in the Passion Translation, I was caught off guard and impacted in a way that is hard to explain. Read it, and see what you think:

> Lord, You know all my desires and deepest longings.
> My tears are liquid words,
> and You can read each one.

I went to a women's retreat years ago where the speaker shared some interesting science about tears. The chemical makeup of our tears varies according to the trigger or emotion behind them. Tears may come from peeling an onion, anger or frustration, physical pain, grief, nostalgia, relief or laughter, and they all look different under a microscope.

But our good, good Father God doesn't need a microscope, and He doesn't need to examine our tears to know what is causing them. He takes the time to "read each one." I don't know about you, but I believe my tears in certain times—especially after Rebekah's murder—spoke *volumes* to God that I could not express in words. Grief, horror, pain, regret, sorrow, frustration, anger, utter brokenness. . .

He cares enough not to let one tear fall without His understanding, compassion, and love welling up as He sees us. Don't let that escape you: He *sees* us! Even when no one else does. He sees the hurt that no one else can see. He sees it in minute detail, knowing every factor involved, and meets us in the pit of despair, sits with us, cradles us so close to His heart that He is able to capture our tears.

How close do you have to be to catch someone's tears in a bottle? How much must you love them, how attentive must you be? How precious must they be to you?

I remember asking my sister Reneé, at some point after Rebekah's death, if she thought people could look at me and know that my daughter had been killed. The truth of the matter is that no one truly knows the anguish in our hearts. Not our closest friends, not even our spouses, if we have one. Not another soul on earth knows completely the depth of pain and grief you have endured, the sleepless nights, the endless flood of tears shed in isolation.

But God does! And He cares about your tears. He keeps track of all our hurts from the day we are born. He has a book written about us, and within the pages are all the sorrows we have endured. Some we may not even remember; some others would discount as unimportant, immature, or the result of our own foolishness. But God sees, cares, and remains with us through each and every one.

Not only is God with us in the pit, but He is also completely aware of our anguish, and He hurts with and for us. We must hold on to this truth, even when we are unable to see God's hand in our circumstances.

The Easter after Rebekah's murder found me unable to get through a single day without tremendous grief. Case in point: Easter—such a blessed, happy time! It is a season in which we focus on our risen Savior. Because of the cross, because He paid the penalty for our sins, and because He rose triumphant over death, hell, and the grave, we are assured eternal life in Him.

Despite my certain belief that Rebekah was with Jesus, I remember going to our church's Palm Sunday service, at which we walked the Stations of the Cross, quite literally bent over with the heaviness of deep, deep sorrow.

We now remember Jesus's suffering and death on Good Friday at our church, and it remains a most impactful experience all these years later. But that Sunday was my first experience with the Stations of the Cross. The congregation moved from one station to another, in no particular order, waiting quietly for our turn at each. Suddenly, the music ceased. As I recall, only the sharp retort of hammer upon nail rang through the sanctuary, coming from the station where we repent of a specific sin as we pound a spike into wood.

David and I moved from one station to another. I can't tell you what I looked like, but I imagine I was more or less shuffling along. I do know that tears were streaming down my face and that I was holding myself very tight. All my muscles were taut, as they pretty much always were at this time. Even in bed, I would find myself stiff and would have to remind myself again and again to relax. It didn't matter what I told myself; before I knew it, I was all tight again.

About halfway through the stations, we came to the one that represents when the soldiers offered Jesus bitter vinegar on a sponge when He was thirsty. The instructions were to dip a cotton swab into the bowl of vinegar, place it on your tongue, and thank God for being with you in the bitter times of life.

I remember so clearly picking up the cotton swab, dipping it in the vinegar, tasting it, and pleading in my mind, "Hold me, Jesus, hold me."

I then experienced something that I had never, and have never again, experienced. I literally, physically felt the presence of the Holy Spirit. I felt what I can only describe as a liquid warmth flowing from my head downward. I felt every muscle in my body relax. And the tears that had been relentlessly flowing the whole time stopped totally, through no volition of my own.

I can't even begin to describe the absolute peace and security that engulfed me. The certainty I felt was that God was with me. He saw me. He was indeed carrying me! It was a genuine miracle in which God revealed the truth that He will never leave or forsake us. He does uphold us with His victorious right hand.

As we moved on to other stations, the physical presence of the Holy Spirit faded. The warmth receded, and tears began to flow again. By the time we were seated, I assume I was once again tense, although I cannot remember that for certain. I only remember everything good that I could feel with my senses dissipating. And yet . . . I knew then, and I know now, that God is within me! God's hands are indeed holding me and helping me. The lack of physically being able to feel the Lord's presence does not negate the reality of it!

I have just begun to memorize Psalm 46:5. This verse refers to a city in its proper context. But the Holy Spirit, God Himself, dwells within me; therefore, I believe those of us who follow Jesus can apply it and be encouraged by its truth: "God is within her, she will not fall. God will help her at the break of day."

The Holy Spirit is real! He is God who is within those of us who belong to Jesus. He is our Comforter (John 14:16); He is our Guide (Romans 8:14); He teaches us (1 Corinthians 2:10–14); He helps us in our weakness and intercedes for us with groans (Romans 8:26). While I never felt that liquid warmth again, while my body never miraculously "melted" again, while my tears never dried in an instant, replaced with an impossible to describe peace, I knew the Holy Spirit was as present with me at all times as He was when I was given the gift of physically feeling His presence.

God is with us! God is in us! Always! We can take great comfort in this during the storms of life, knowing that we are not walking through them on our own. There is Someone who genuinely sees all of us. He literally knows all we have gone through, are going through, and will go through. And He will walk with us no matter what the future holds.

Chapter 10
When You Can't See God

After being married for only a few years, I remember sitting with David's family for dinner at the home he grew up in. It was always a treat to eat his mom's good cooking, and I so enjoyed any time with her, David's dad, and his sisters. As I remember, it was David's mom and dad; Susan, his older sister, who had only been married about a year longer than us; and his little sister, Beth.

At some point, and for some reason, the conversation moved to a woman who had lost her husband in a terrible accident. To spare her the trauma of seeing his body, they had allowed her to identify him by looking at his hand.

David's mom stated emphatically that she knew she could recognize her husband by just his hand. Susan, although only married a short time, agreed that she could also recognize her husband by his hand alone. I sat, thought for a moment, and then confessed that I wasn't sure I could recognize David just by looking at his hand. All conversation ceased, and everyone stared at me. I could feel my face heating in embarrassment and imagined they were appalled that my love could be so shallow. I don't remember who said, "Really? You couldn't recognize him by his hands?"

You see, when David was two years old, he had fallen onto a floor furnace, suffering third- and fourth-degree burns on the palms of his hands. He'd had multiple surgeries and skin grafts as his hands grew but the grafted skin did not. One of his thumbs is slightly deformed because the heat damaged the bone.

I had completely forgotten all this as I tried to figure out if I could indeed recognize David by his hands alone. Truth be told, I never thought about David's scars or even "saw" them. In contemplating the question, I failed to remember the unique distinguishing features of my husband's hands! I thought I couldn't recognize them, but the truth was that I definitely could. Everyone at the table had a great laugh as they saw the "light" flip on in my mind, and then I laughed too!

God *is* with us in times of horrific tragedy, pain, loss, and suffering. But there are times when those heavy drapes—or our own forgetfulness or wrong thinking—conceal His presence.

The good news is that God wants us to see His hand at work in our lives! "Praise the LORD, for He has shown me the wonders of His unfailing love" (Psalm 31:21a).

God reveals His hand to us so that we can see how much He loves us and how faithful He is. But it's not always (and unfortunately, to our way of thinking, very rare) that He reveals Himself the moment we are thrust down into that old pit of despair.

Not only does our grief and the mud and mire of our situation blind us, but we have an enemy who is desperately trying to convince us that we are indeed alone! That God either never knew us, never cared for us, is powerless to help us, or has simply walked away and left us to fend for ourselves. (Please contrast those lies with the image of Jesus, our Good Shepherd, leaving the ninety-nine to chase after the one in Matthew 18:12.) Or that God is the one who put us in that pit to begin with—to punish us, to teach us a lesson, or simply because the pit is where He wants us to be.

Let's look at the traps we find ourselves in when trying to recognize God's hand and how to escape them.

Trap 1: We question God's character and intentions for us and our loved ones.

Who God is and what He does are irrevocably linked. What God does reveals His character. So if the enemy of our souls can convince us that God has abandoned us, even for a moment, or if he can cause us to doubt the utter goodness and love of our heavenly Father, he can effectively cause great distortion about who we perceive God to be.

Sitting in that most awful pit, we can begin to question God's character and intentions. We can fail to recognize His hand of love and even attribute terrible, unloving things to Him.

Several years ago, when I was on staff at my church, we took a trip to New York for a conference. We all met at the church at 4:00 a.m., and after a comedy of errors and plane issues held us up in airports or on planes for sixteen and a half hours, we finally arrived safely in New York.

The fearless leader of our group waited in line for our rental car, and soon he was driving us to the hotel.

The time was around 8:30 p.m., and it was dark, but the roads were well lit. Our leader and another man were in the front seats, and I was scrunched in with two other ladies in the back. As we drove, a car pulled up alongside ours on the driver's side. The driver rolled his window down and made motions with his free hand while steering with the other and mouthing something we couldn't hear or understand.

I was seated on the passenger side, so my three dear coworkers saw him before I did. We thought he wanted us to roll down our windows. One person instructed our driver, "Don't look at him!" A toll plaza loomed up ahead. The other said, "He wants us to throw him money!" We were exhausted, in an unfamiliar place, and a bit taken aback by this crazy guy in the vehicle next to us. What would he do if we didn't give him money for the toll?

Our fearless leader finally realized that the poor guy was trying to tell us our headlights weren't on! It had been so bright in the rental car lot and then on the road that we hadn't even noticed. In this case, we had seen the man's hand but, not knowing his character, we had misjudged his intent.

It is so important that we get to know God intimately. This is how we escape the trap of misjudging God's character and intentions.

How important it is that we come to know that God is utterly and completely good. As are His intentions for us. He is not like an earthly father who may abandon or abuse. God is even better than a wonderful earthly father who loves with all his heart but who is imperfect, makes mistakes, and fails at times.

After my father was diagnosed with colon cancer, he began having terrible headaches. He, my mom, and I headed to the VA hospital in Salem, Virginia, where they admitted him to do a brain scan. When my mom and I left the hospital that evening and headed to our hotel, she said, "Perhaps God will be merciful and the cancer will not be in Daddy's brain."

Now I'm not picking on my mom. But can you see the errors in her thinking? First: "*Perhaps* God will be merciful." Is God merciful or not to His people? God is a God of mercy. Mercy is part of who He is! Yes, He is also perfectly just, but this was not a situation in which justice came into play. God's character is such that He is never unmerciful to His children.

Second: Mama linked God's mercy to the cancer not being in Daddy's brain, which would mean that if the cancer were in Daddy's brain, God was not merciful. The reason I share this is because it is so easy—for even those of us with years of solid biblical teaching and guidance, years of following Jesus, years of loving Jesus and knowing Him—when we are in a desperate situation to question God's character if our prayers are not answered a certain way or the outcome of a situation is, to be blunt, absolutely horrible.

That evening, I gently said to my mother, "Oh, Mama, God is *always* merciful." She quite readily agreed. She just needed to be reminded of what she already knew.

We can certainly look back to remind ourselves of God's goodness and faithfulness in the past, thanking and praising

Him out loud. Hand in hand with our thankfulness and praise is our knowledge of, meditation on, and memorization of God's Word.

Remember, causing us to doubt God's character and intentions toward us is a tool of the devil. And the most powerful weapons against the enemy are our praise and God's Word spoken aloud. Spend time basking in the truths of God's Word when down in that cold, miserable pit of despair!

Psalm 145:17: "The LORD is righteous in everything He does; he is filled with kindness."

Jeremiah 29:11: "'For I know the plans I have for you,' says the LORD. 'They are plans for good and not for disaster, to give you a future and a hope.'"

Psalm 103:1–6, 8, 10–14:

> Let all that I am praise the LORD;
> with my whole heart, I will praise his holy name.
> Let all that I am praise the LORD;
> may I never forget the good things he does for me.
> He forgives all my sins
> and heals all my diseases.
> He redeems me from death
> and crowns me with love and tender mercies.
> He fills my life with good things.
> My youth is renewed like the eagle's!
> The LORD gives righteousness
> and justice to all who are treated unfairly.
> The LORD is compassionate and merciful,
> slow to get angry and filled with unfailing love.
> He will not constantly accuse us,
> nor remain angry forever.
> He does not punish us for all our sins;

> he does not deal harshly with us, as we deserve.
> For his unfailing love toward those who fear him
> is as great as the height of the heavens above the earth.
> He has removed our sins as far from us
> as the east is from the west.
> The LORD is like a father to his children,
> tender and compassionate to those who fear him.
> For he knows how weak we are;
> he remembers we are only dust.

I could use the rest of this book sharing scriptures that accurately reveal God's heart for us and His unchanging character! Spend time in His Word. Use a Bible app or Google or the scriptures in the back of this book to find verses that comfort, encourage, and deeply impact you.

Lastly, to escape this trap of questioning God's character and love for you, get to know Jesus! Read the gospels. Why?

- "Christ is the visible image of the invisible God" (Colossians 1:15a).
- "The Son radiates God's own glory and expresses the very character of God" (Hebrews 1:3a).
- As Jesus said, "I tell you the truth, the Son can do nothing by himself. He does only what he sees the Father doing. Whatever the Father does the Son also does" (John 5:19).
- And just before John 5:19 is one of my favorite verses: "The Father is always working and so am I" (John 5:17).

Read the gospels! Jesus reveals God's character; He reveals how God feels toward us and looks at us. Jesus heals, brings life, forgives, and shows compassion, grace, and mercy even when He corrects.

God longs for us to *know* Him so intimately and *trust* Him so completely that it would never even occur to us to blame Him for what is wrong in our lives and in our world. Rather than turning away with feelings of abandonment and accusation, He longs for us to run to Him for whatever it is we need: comfort, courage, strength, mercy, forgiveness, grace, wisdom, understanding . . . *love* . . . in the midst of our difficulties, tragedies, and agonies.

Trap 2: We focus on our circumstances and fail to see God's hand.

This is not unique to us! Chapters 14–17 of Exodus clearly show what the Israelites focused on when God was delivering them from Egypt and guiding them through the wilderness.

They complained about everything! When trapped by the Red Sea: "Were there not enough graves in Egypt?" When water was bitter: "What are we going to drink?" When food was scarce: "We will starve to death!" When no water (not even bitter water) was to be found: "You (Moses) are trying to kill us, our children, and our livestock with thirst!"

God had performed, and continued every step of the way to perform, mighty miracles on their behalf. But with each new crisis, His people could focus on nothing but their circumstances and long, not for the things of God, but for all they had left behind in Egypt. Egypt . . . where they may have had melons to eat but were enslaved and robbed of their children. Oh, how quickly they—and we—forget!

How do we escape this trap? I think it's two-fold: a looking *back* and a looking *up*.

We look back, remembering and focusing on God's faithfulness and goodness to us in the past. Psalm 11:4 says, "He causes us to remember his wonderful works." We need to look back to when it was easier to recognize how God was with us and His hand was working for us.

And then, we look up, having faith that our God, who never changes and never stops working, is working for us now, just as He did then.

The Bible is filled with stories of the Israelites looking back over their time in the wilderness. From the vantage point of being outside those circumstances, they clearly and vividly saw God's hand. How He worked for them, even while they complained! He parted the Red Sea, brought them through on dry ground, and drowned the enemy Egyptian army that was pursuing them. He made bitter water sweet. He fed them manna and quail. He brought water out of rocks. For forty years, their clothes and shoes did not wear out. And so on and so on.

As they remembered, they looked up to God with great gratitude and renewed trust in His character and hope for their current situation.

The day Rebekah was murdered, I was unable to see God's hand in the midst of a trauma that made it difficult to function, much less breathe. But looking back now, I could write pages and pages about all the ways God worked on David's and my behalf that day. This would become a book of epic proportions if I tried to share just a fraction of all the ways my good, good Father's hand moved for my benefit, not only that day but also in the weeks, months, and years to come. I didn't see everything then. I can see so much more clearly now. And I am sure there are countless ways God has intervened for my sake that I will never know until I get to heaven.

Look back! Look up! Ask the Holy Spirit to help you see and remember His goodness in the past. Remember that He is still working. Ask Him for faith in the present moment, in which you cannot see.

"So we don't look at the troubles we can see now; rather, we fix our gaze on things that cannot be seen. For the things we see now will soon be gone, but the things we cannot see will last forever" (2 Corinthians 4:18).

Trap 3: We are impatient.

This trap is huge! At least for me. I want to push through seasons of difficulty as quickly as possible. All too often, we can be so fixed on what we want the final outcome of our situation to be that we miss the ways God is working along the way. All we can think is "I'm still dealing with _____. I'm still hurting. I'm still waiting, God! Where are You?"

And if you are like me, the only thing to do in such a situation, when God seems to be poking along, is to "help" Him. I cringe to think of all the times I have failed to see God working on my behalf or on behalf of those I love because I was impatient. I have tried to manipulate situations, and even worse, people . . . but all with the best intentions, of course! I have tried to force *my* timetable and deadlines on the Lord of all Creation.

Do you know what impatience leads to? Without fail? Every time? *Disobedience.* We displease God with our attitudes and thoughts, even if our impatience doesn't lead to taking action on our part. Doubt, unkindness, manipulation, accusation, rash decisions, taking control of things we have no business taking control of, trying to force what we want when we want it (it's what's best, after all . . . right?). All of it: disobedience.

And here's a most sobering thought: Our disobedience can hinder all the good God wants to do in and for us and for those we love. Impatience is ugly, damaging, and ungodly.

How do we break free from this insidious trap that is so much a part of our culture of convenience these days? We ask for more patience. We pray and plead with God to give us more.

But patience doesn't come out of nowhere. It has a Source. If I want ready access to apples, I plant an apple tree. And if I want more apples, I need more of the source of apples: apple trees. I cannot just expect the one tree I have to produce a truckload of more apples. That is a fruitless hope (pardon the pun).

Patience comes as a fruit of the Holy Spirit living inside us. If we want more fruit (patience), we pray for more of the source of that fruit, which is the Holy Spirit. And this is a prayer that delights the Lord. He loves to give us more of Himself!

We ask for more of the Holy Spirit, and then . . . we wait on Him. And as we wait, we choose to believe that God is working. He will rescue, help, strengthen, redeem. If we wait on God with a patient heart and thoughts that are not anxiously scattered, trying to get God to move a little faster, we are much better able to see His hand along the way.

Here are some wonderful verses about waiting:

- Psalm 62:5: "Let all that I am wait quietly before God, for my hope is in him."
- Psalm 37:7a: "Be still in the presence of the LORD and wait patiently for him to act."
- Psalm 46:10a: "Be still, and know that I am God!"
- And my very favorite, Isaiah 64:4: "For since the world be-

gan, no ear has heard and no eye has seen a God like you, who works for those who wait on him!"

Let's explore what "waiting" on the Lord looks like. I'm sure you've heard sayings like "God doesn't move parked cars." There is some truth in this. Every situation we find ourselves in will be unique, and I believe we should seek the Lord and perhaps consult godly counsel as to exactly what our waiting patiently and quietly in each situation entails.

Here is a story that has helped me over the years. One of the times we were visiting my parents in Warm Springs, Georgia, there was a threat of a tornado. Alarms sounded, and we all scurried to prepare. Adults moved vehicles under the portico, and we instructed the children to bring all their toys inside. We moved the outdoor furniture that we could inside and had flashlights handy. We might have worked for thirty minutes, and we were hustling.

Then, we all sat down at the dining room table to have dinner. Little Davy, who might have been as old as twelve, looked at us dumbfounded. "You mean we're just going to sit here and eat?" he exclaimed incredulously.

"Well, yes, Buddy," I said. "We've done everything we can and know how to do. Now we pray, ask God to take care of everything we can't, and have a good evening."

And we did! The tornado struck not too far from us, but as I remember it, there were no fatalities and not a great deal of damage, thank the Lord.

I believe God gave me those words to tell Davy. And I believe they are an accurate example we can follow in a lot of situations. If I need a job, I don't pray, then sit at home watching TV. I make calls, fill out résumés, ask friends if they know of anyone who is hiring, and so on. I do what I can do and then ask God to provide a good job for me. And when I get one, I thank Him!

Are you in a relationship that is concerning you or those who love God and you? Read God's Word. Do not let the Bible fall open and point at a verse randomly but rather search the Scriptures and allow God to reveal His truth and His will. Seek out godly counsel about this relationship.

Are you between a rock and a hard place, and the only way out seems to be to set aside your moral convictions and integrity? Choose the hard way: honesty, integrity, and obedience to God because you fear only Him. Then wait for God to keep His promises and work on your behalf.

Think back to our story about Shadrach, Meshach, and Abednego. Or Joseph, betrayed by his brothers and suffering in an Egyptian prison for years, waiting on God.

So what does waiting on God look like? Because we have placed our hope in God, and because hope brings peace and joy, our waiting should not be the pace-the-floor, anxious kind. Neither is it a prop-your-feet-up and take-a-nap kind of waiting. We do our part and *then* . . . we wait.

We wait from a position of surrendered obedience. This obedience is what activates God's promises to us. "Make thankfulness your sacrifice to God and keep the vows you have made to the Most High. Then call on me when you are in trouble, and I will rescue you, and you will give me glory" (Psalm 50:14–15).

1. We set aside our desire to control and manipulate others and circumstances.
2. We set aside our tendency to want to nudge God or give directions or time frames within which we demand He work.
3. We commit to being thankful, searching for things to be thankful for, in the midst of the most devastating storms.

I also love Psalm 5:3 (NIV): "In the morning, LORD, you hear my voice; in the morning I lay my requests before you and wait expectantly."

In our waiting, there is also a surrender—a laying down of our burdens, fears, anxieties, preferences, imaginings, and pride. May I go so far as to say a laying down of our desires, although we can hold our desires "loosely"?

As I wrote that, I wondered exactly what it looks like. When David was a UPS driver, he was taught how to hand a box to a child. He was not to simply hand it over, for they might not be strong enough to hold it. He was to hold the box on open palms and extend it to the child. Should the box be too heavy, David's hands would be positioned to catch the box, keeping it from falling to the ground.

When we surrender our desires to God, we are the child in this scenario. We long to receive and carry and possess whatever is in our box. We ask God for it, but we trust Him to know what is truly best for us and to keep His hands underneath not only our desire but also underneath us!

Perhaps that desire is what He longs for us too. In that case, we are able to receive and enjoy it fully. Perhaps He knows that our desire includes something that is "too heavy" for us, such as a long-term consequence we are unaware of. Perhaps

He has a better alternative that is His best for us. Perhaps it's a reason that we will never completely understand, but we can choose to trust in our good, good Father, despite our lack of understanding. Nevertheless, we can lay our desires before the Lord, trusting He will work for what is best for us.

And then there is the waiting! We wait *expectantly*. To be expectant is to look forward to with—wait for it—*hope* that something good is coming! We do not wait with worry or dread. Although they may creep in, we recognize them and refuse to let them remain our driving emotions.

We surrender those boxes. We surrender our very lives, and we obey. We do what we can do, what He would have us to do, and then we hope in Him and quiet ourselves before Him, waiting for Him to work on our behalf.

And speaking of boxes. . .

Trap 4: We try to put God in a box.

Have you ever felt you needed to tell God what to do? And how to do it? And what the final result should look like? And how long it should take? And . . . and . . . ?

We usually have a picture in our minds of how things should go. Because we are so smart, you know! We show God the blueprint, give Him our marching orders, and then wait, sometimes even patiently, for Him to fix everything to our specifications.

I was only seven years old when my daddy was shot down in Vietnam. His life was miraculously spared (another story for another time), but he was paralyzed from the waist down from a bullet that severed his spinal column. Infinitely worse than being paralyzed was the excruciating pain he suffered. The bullet also frayed nerve endings that sent pain impulses to his brain twenty-four seven. Daddy was always in pain. *Always.* The pain would, multiple times a day, increase in intensity until he would scream. On cloudy, stormy days or when he was sick or had an infection, the pain would be such that he could only lie in bed, crying and shrieking in agony.

A seven-year-old does not understand the implications of severed spinal cords and frayed nerve endings. All I knew was that my daddy was hurting. My mom shared years later that she would sometimes find me under my bed, on Daddy's worst days, crying. I prayed for his healing. For God to take away his pain. I believed God could do it! And yet the pain persisted.

Mama says there came a day when I asked in frustration and hurt, "Why isn't God answering our prayers for Daddy?" In great wisdom, surely given by the Holy Spirit, she answered while holding me in her arms, "Oh, Nancy Jo, God *is* answering our prayers! He is giving your daddy strength to get through each day." She was wise enough to see God's hand outside the box of the complete healing we prayed for.

In the late 1970s, Daddy was spotlighted in an article on pain in *Newsweek*. At the time, he was one of only three people in the world known to endure this level of pain. His many failed attempts to find relief included a dorsal column implant that sent electrical impulses to his spine and gave only limited relief for the constant pain and no relief for the elevated pain. He also agreed to an alcohol block, which is an injection of alcohol or phenol to anesthetize damaged nerves. (Thank the Lord they tried a numbing medication first, for the moment the injection hit those frayed nerves, Daddy's body reacted in a convulsion that caused the drugs to spill over so that he could not sit up or breathe without help until they wore off.)

It was twenty-three years after Daddy was injured that he finally got relief. For some reason, as he aged, the pain escalated to higher intensities and greater frequencies. Before his thirteen-hour surgery, when they cauterized all the frayed nerves, Daddy was taking the highest dose of blood-pressure medication he could safely tolerate, and his blood pressure was still at stroke level. After the surgery, which completely eliminated the excruciating pain—praise God!—he was paralyzed at a higher point, but his blood pressure returned to normal with zero medication, and he never had trouble with it again.

Twenty-three years of excruciating pain . . . Only God knows how he lived with it all those years. I have found myself wishing I could ask his input for this book—to share how he maintained hope through those many years of unimaginable pain. I wish I could share his insights with you. One thing I know for certain is that he would credit God with giving him the strength to endure. One of Daddy's favorite Bible verses was "But he said to me, 'My grace is sufficient for you, for my power is made perfect in weakness.' Therefore I will boast all the more gladly about my weaknesses, so that Christ's power may rest on me" (2 Corinthians 12:9 NIV).

I also know he would have said it is important to have a purpose, to have as much fun as possible, and to focus on loving others. Hopelessness has a way of causing us to fold into ourselves, to become self-focused and self-absorbed. This is a very dangerous place to be, for it simply feeds whatever thoughts are stealing hope from us. When we feel the most hopeless, we must get outside of ourselves.

Daddy chose to surround himself with positive people who loved God and who enjoyed life. Yes, he cried and screamed in agony. But the sound I remember most was his boisterous, contagious laugh! He was humble enough to laugh at himself, and he taught me to do the same. (More on that later!) He was in the Word consistently, and more so as he aged. He worked hard and played hard too. He enjoyed crafts, hunting, eating, telling and listening to stories, and teaching me, everything from plumbing to diving, bowling, driving, and more. He was one of the most forgiving, gracious, generous people I have ever known. And along with a love for God and family, I believe it was hope that nurtured these qualities. Hope for help here on earth, yes. But more than that, it was the absolute, certain hope that he would one day be pain-free, able to walk again, and perfectly healthy in every way for all eternity.

Daddy was diagnosed with colon cancer in 2003, which had spread outside the colon wall before they found it. The cancer rapidly metastasized to his brain, lung, and liver before he died on December 3, 2004. As with the battle against pain, Daddy fought the cancer battle with the same hope *in* God. He most certainly hoped *for* healing, as did we all. And he did all he could to help himself.

Throughout the immensely difficult battle, he retained that same perspective with which he endured pain. He always focused on others. I will never forget riding with him in an ambulance, from one hospital to another, with a surly EMT sitting with us. Although very sick, Daddy tried so hard to engage the man and brighten his day. I vividly remember sitting in a waiting room at the VA hospital as Daddy listened to a man share about his ministry and then gave him money for the ministry. Daddy also wanted to be sure that Mama would have everything she needed. He loved to buy things for me and others. He never allowed self-centeredness to rob him of the joy of blessing others, even in the most desperate and awful of times.

Daddy's bout with cancer was honestly horrible. I still grieve the pain he suffered through it and the death process. But I cling to this image: Although Daddy had been unresponsive for two to three days, although he labored all night long to breathe, his face frozen and impassive, upon his final breath, he wore a *smile*! I could not, and still cannot, get over it. A genuine, gentle smile graced his dear face. How could this be?

I can only share this verse from Romans 8: "Yet what we suffer now is nothing compared to the glory he will reveal to us later. For all creation is waiting eagerly for that future day when God will reveal who his children really are" (vv. 18–19). There is no way to adequately convey the suffering I know my father endured. There is no way I can truly understand the depth and length of suffering, even though I witnessed it. Therefore, there is no way I — *we* — can possibly begin to grasp the glory that awaits us in heaven in the presence of God Himself! I believe with all my heart that Daddy caught a glimpse of that glory when stepping from this world into eternity and that his face reflected what we can only dream of.

It is this sure and certain hope of heaven, of life with God in His loving presence that carries us through hell on earth. The truth is that this is *not* all there is, praise God! That even a hundred-year-long life on earth is but a tiny blip on the unending timeline of eternity. It is the mighty power of God that lives within us through the Holy Spirit that enables us to endure unimaginable suffering and "hopeless" circumstances filled with the hope of heaven!

I am utterly convinced that it was the power of the Holy Spirit within him that kept my father from committing suicide amid those unending days, weeks, months, and years of unrelenting pain. I will never forget hearing him confess to another man, who had shared that an acquaintance of theirs had tried to commit suicide, that he understood getting to that point of giving up. Again, I so wish I could ask Daddy to share with us exactly what enabled him to overcome that temptation. But whatever other insights he would point us to, I wholeheartedly believe that Daddy's ability to survive—and not only survive but also *thrive*—through twenty-three years of pain is a testimony of how great, how powerful, how faithful, and how mighty the power of the Holy Spirit who lives within us is!

Hezekiah's prayer when the Assyrian army threatened to invade Israel is a powerful example of how to pray. I love this story (2 Kings 19–22) and encourage you to read it for yourself. The king of Assyria had threatened to destroy Israel like he had the surrounding nations in a letter that was delivered to Hezekiah. Hezekiah locked himself in the Lord's house and lay the letter out on the floor. Then he prayed in 2 Kings 19:15–19:

> O Lord, God of Israel, you are enthroned between the mighty cherubim! You alone are God of all the kingdoms of the earth. You alone created the heavens and the earth. Bend down, O Lord, and listen! Open your eyes, O Lord, and see! Listen to Sennacherib's words of defiance against the living God.
>
> It is true, Lord, that the kings of Assyria have destroyed all these nations. And they have thrown the gods of these nations into the fire and burned them. But of course the Assyrians could destroy them! They were not gods at all—only idols of wood and stone shaped by human hands. Now, O Lord our God, rescue us from his power; then all the kingdoms of the earth will know that you alone, O Lord, are God.

Hezekiah went straight to the Lord with the trouble. He laid it out before God. This is evidence that Hezekiah knew God could see everything. He let God "read" the letter for Himself. (I can waste a lot of prayer time unnecessarily explaining situations to God. I wonder how many times I'm even accurate in my explanations from such a limited perspective.)

After spreading the letter out on the ground, Hezekiah acknowledged who God is and gave Him glory. He was going before God the Creator, God Almighty, the One and Only True God, and the God who sees and hears all that transpires down here on earth.

Hezekiah did not fail to address the truth in the letter of the victories Assyria had claimed over all the other nations. But he also spoke aloud the truth that victory over those nations was inevitable because they didn't have the help of the One True God.

Then, Hezekiah simply makes his request for rescue. He does not tell God how or when. He trusts God to figure that out. And—this is so important—he desires not only rescue but also that God be recognized as the One True God and receive all the glory and praise.

Later, we find God's rescue to go beyond what Hezekiah could have possibly imagined. And it left no room for anyone to take credit or praise other than God Himself (vv. 35–36):

> That night the angel of the LORD went out to the Assyrian camp and killed 185,000 Assyrian soldiers. When the surviving Assyrians woke up the next morning, they found corpses everywhere. Then King Sennacherib of Assyria broke camp and returned to his own land. He went home to his capital of Nineveh and stayed there.

I prayed for my daughter, Rebekah, from the moment I knew she was growing inside me. And when she was killed, I was really confused. I cried out to God one day in my living room, "Lord! Did You even hear my prayers for her? Because it sure doesn't seem like You did!" In no way, shape, or form did Rebekah's murder fit into the box I had handed to God.

The Holy Spirit impressed upon my heart to get out my prayer journals and reread my recorded prayers for Rebekah. As I read my journal entries from the previous year, I found that my prayers for my daughter fit into four different main requests:

1. *That God would set her free from the sin she was caught up in.* And He did! Rebekah is enjoying heaven without having to deal with a sin nature ever again. She does not struggle with sin. She is not even tempted! (I think that after seeing Jesus, Rebekah, Daddy, and other loved ones and never grieving again, this is one of the things I look forward to the most in heaven.)
2. *That God would draw her to Him.* He did! Rebekah is in the very presence of God Himself. She is beholding Jesus face to face. She now knows how much He loves her.
3. *That God would safeguard her life.* This one gave me pause. But as I wrestled with it, the Lord revealed this truth to me: God safeguarded Rebekah's life the moment she decided to accept Jesus as Savior and Lord. Although in her youth and adulthood, she veered off the narrow road, she never turned her back on God. She longed to be free from all that bound her and to be able to be a good witness to others. I don't think she ever had a friend for long with whom she did not share Jesus.
4. *Lastly, that God would use Rebekah to build His kingdom.* It was up to me to put feet to this prayer. I have shared Rebekah's story in prisons, in women's shelters, in churches, at GriefShare meetings, with neighbors, friends, and even strangers who sometimes became friends. Rebekah's story, her struggles, and all my failures are being used in all their

imperfections to build God's kingdom, to point others to Him and help them see that God is good—always!

How do we get out of this trap of boxing God in? We begin by confessing it as sin and repenting.

Isaiah 40:13–14 (NIV):

> Who can fathom the Spirit of the LORD, or instruct the LORD as his counselor? Whom did the LORD consult to enlighten him, and who taught him the right way? Who was it that taught him knowledge, or showed him the path of understanding?

How embarrassing and humiliating to realize I—a sinful, mortal, weak, human being who is limited in perspective and time—thought God needed directions and counsel from me. How arrogant and prideful!

We must ask God to forgive us for this sin and ask the Holy Spirit to alert us if we fall into this trap again. Because it *is* a trap! We must not limit God, and we must not tell Him how to do things.

Isaiah 55:8–9:

> "My thoughts are nothing like your thoughts," says the LORD. "And my ways are far beyond anything you could imagine. For just as the heavens are higher than the earth, so my ways are higher than your ways and my thoughts higher than your thoughts."

God does not feel obligated to follow our plans. And you know, I am so thankful for this! Paul is so on target in Romans 8 when he says that we don't even know how to pray. Our perspective is so limited, our motives are so tainted, our desires are so fickle.

The entire time I was pregnant with Davy, I prayed that God would let me deliver naturally and not surgically. It was an almost daily, heartfelt plea that expressed the deepest desire of my heart. Better for the baby, better for me. Better all the way around. Surely God would hear my fervent prayers. I ate right, gained minimal weight, and exercised almost daily.

I went into labor on Sunday, October 7. Intense labor did not begin until mid-afternoon on Monday, October 8. Somewhere between then and ten o'clock that night when Davy was born, my prayer became a cry of desperation for the doctor to come and declare that I *needed* a C-section! *Anything* to stop the pain. Can't you just see the Lord grinning? A gentle grin, full of compassion and love, but a grin nonetheless.

And here's maybe the most wonderful news of all: We can count on God's good plans always being birthed, even when His will is not done. It was not God's will for Rebekah to be murdered (remember God's character and intentions). And yet, when He pointed me back to those prayer journals, I realized that He had indeed answered every single one of my prayers. Would I have preferred to see those prayers answered differently? Oh, yes! My heart still cries "Yes!" to that question. But the reality is that my hopes and dreams *for* Rebekah were not fulfilled the way I pictured.

We do get to choose whether or not to cooperate with the Lord. But when we choose to surrender to Him, and we look outside any boxes we might be holding on tight to, we can see His hand of love and His faithfulness.

We must ask the Holy Spirit to help us see outside the box. Even better, we must throw away our boxes and simply trust

God to work for our good and His glory without our instructions. Imagine that!

Trap 5: We fail to recognize God's hand in the good.

We take the good in our lives for granted, failing to recognize God's loving hand as the author of *every* good thing we have (James 1:17). We go through days of good health, financial stability, intact families, safe travel . . . and never think twice about thanking God for His generous gifts. We overcome addictions, unforgiveness, and bitterness; we enjoy restored relationships; yet we forget that it is God who gives us the desire and the power to do what pleases Him.

Yes, we have a role to play in all of this. We take care of our bodies, lose weight, spend wisely, love well, drive defensively (*very* defensively these days), choose to go to rehab, forgive, and so on. But it is God who supplies every breath we need. It is God who gives us wisdom and helps us to love the hard to love, to stay true to our spouse, to afford good food and rehab and counseling and so on. Yes, we go to school, but did we create our brains? Who placed us in a country where we can get a good education? Who gave us parents who loved us and/or protected us? There is no good thing that we cannot trace back to the kind, merciful, generous, loving hand of God.

But we get so busy with life and all the good things we have that we simply don't pause to think about how blessed we are. I'm terrible about this with my poor husband. I'll bring up a chore he neglects, such as picking up his socks. I'll ask nicely. I'll explain how it annoys me. While holding up a pair of dirty socks, I'll ask a passive-aggressive question like "Are these clean?" You get the idea. Then, one day out of the blue, he'll ask me, "Have you noticed you haven't had to pick up my socks lately?"

"Uh . . . no," I'll admit with a cringe, an "I'm sorry," and a "Thank you!"

Remember COVID? Every day that I was not sick, I thanked the Lord for my good health, as people all around us were falling ill. I'll do the same after I've had the flu or some illness or surgery. I will be so grateful when I'm feeling better and able to function and enjoy life again. But after a while of good health, I begin to forget to be thankful.

How do we avoid this trap? By actively looking and giving thanks for the good in our lives.

Daddy taught me the "Thank You Game." Whenever something bad, inconvenient, or even terrible happens, you look for everything you can thank God for. This may be even in the most trivial of circumstances. Just the other day, as I took my mug of tea out of the microwave to reheat it, I caught the mug on the edge of the oven and sloshed tea everywhere. I was *not* happy. But falling into that wonderful habit Daddy instilled in me, I said out loud, "Lord, I thank You that my mug did not break. I thank You that I had not cleaned the floors yet—in fact, that's on the agenda today. I thank You that I didn't burn myself." That was honestly all I could come up with at that moment, but it was enough. The wave of irritation/aggravation lifted completely!

I challenge you to find a situation in which you cannot find at least one thing to be grateful for. In all my years, I've never not been able to, not even in the case of Rebekah's murder: Police found her body right away. The murderer was caught and never denied killing her. Of all the places this could have happened it was a small town in West Virginia where God set in place the most wonderful victim's advocate, prosecuting attorney, and police sergeant, all working on our behalf. The

Women's Aid in Crisis organization was nearby and gave us its support. Here at home, we were newly situated in a church that was uniquely qualified to love, comfort, and teach us, walking with us through the aftermath.

Do not hear me wrong: The grief was still overwhelming. The anguish was crushing. I was certain that I would literally die from grief. Frustrations with the justice system were a major hurdle. And so much more! *But* thankfulness was a balm to our souls, as we looked for every single thing we could thank the Lord for.

First Thessalonians 5:16–18: "Always be joyful. Never stop praying. Be thankful in all circumstances, for this is God's will for you who belong to Christ Jesus."

Start a gratitude journal. Every day write down at least three things you are thankful for. Studies have shown that gratitude has a positive effect on the attitudes and happiness of people, even non-believers.

What/who are blessings you enjoy? Spouse, parents, children, grandchildren, friends, neighbors? A cup of coffee or tea? (I found a loose-leaf tea company that I thank the Lord for and ask Him to bless almost every morning![3]) Are you healthy? If not, do you have medical care? Are you improving? If you have a terminal illness, do you know for certain where you are going in the end? Can you walk? If you can't walk, do you have a wheelchair? Do you have enough food to eat? Clothes to wear? Do you have friends and family who love you? Do your appliances work? Do you have a good church home? Do you have pets to love and who love you? How about a comfy bed or chair, a cozy blanket, clean linens and towels? Clean hot

---

3. Plum Deluxe Tea: https://www.plumdeluxe.com.

or cold running water at the turn of a knob? Heat in the winter and air conditioning in the summer? A vehicle that runs? Can you read, see, hear, breathe without effort? Did someone smile at you today? Was there someone you were able to bless with a smile or a kind word?

Start your journal today! You will be amazed at how you begin to see things differently. There will be less taking for granted and a more growing appreciation for the multitude of blessings that God pours out upon us daily.

Refuse to fall into the trap of not thanking and praising God for all the good and yet grumbling and even accusing Him or questioning His love when bad things happen. Take me up on this challenge. Play the Thank You Game, start your journal, and see where you are in a month's time. I can almost guarantee that you will be seeing God's hand of love, grace, mercy, and blessing much more clearly.

Although grief no longer consumes me, some days are especially difficult and tears once again flow freely. Rebekah's birthday and the anniversary of her death are two of the hardest days, even now, seventeen years later. On one such day a few years ago, I was really struggling, not only with sadness but also that deep longing for Rebekah to not be forgotten. I honestly cannot remember if it was her birthday or the anniversary of her death, but I had a chiropractor appointment that day. I entered the building, signed in, and sat down near a woman who was wearing a hat. "Nancy Jo?" she tentatively asked.

I looked up and realized it was Rebekah's dearly loved piano teacher, Marsha Berg! She spoke of Rebekah, of her talent, of how she *hated* practicing scales, of how delightful she was, and she said that she thought about Rebekah often. What an incredible gift and example of God going ahead of me! I had never seen Marsha in that office until that day, and I have never run into her there since.

It may be tempting to pass off such experiences as coincidences or luck or something else. But here's the truth: God loves each of us so very, very much. He knows what we need before we do—not just physical needs but heart and soul needs. And something like running into a friend who knew and loved Rebekah and who was kind enough to talk about her to me—for us to be in that waiting room together on the exact day and at the exact time that God knew I needed a little encouragement—*that*, dear readers, is the tender, loving hand of God!

Worship music also helps cultivate gratitude. I enjoy Christian radio, but most of what I hear there is not what I am referring to. I mean songs that focus on who God is—His character. Songs like "Is He Worthy?" "Jesus, Lover of My Soul," "Way Maker," "Crowns Down," "You Are More," among others. Also songs that focus on His promises and our response to who He is such as "Gratitude," "First Things First, "This Is Amazing Grace," "Have My Heart," "Promises," and "I Will Carry You."

You can find a link to these and more songs in the back of the book. Surround yourself with uplifting, truth-filled, scripturally accurate music.

IV.
Trouble

Chapter 11
Hope After Failure

We can hope in God's goodness when misfortune strikes. We can hope in God's faithfulness when others are not faithful. We can hope in our good, good Father to intercede on our behalf amid all sorts of situations that would otherwise suck all hope, joy, and peace right out of us.

But what about when we have failed? What about when the situation we find ourselves in is no one's fault but our own? When we have brought about our own devastating circumstances? Whether it's financial ruin or physical illness caused by poor choices or neglect, an annihilated reputation, or the irrevocable injury or even the death of another. What about when we have sinned, erred, broken God's or man's laws to such an extent that we will reap literal consequences for the rest of our lives? What about when our failure is very public and humiliating? Where is hope to be found in these situations?

This manuscript was finished, or so I thought, when I felt a prompting from the Lord to explore hopelessness in those of us who are left with a crumpled, torn, stained, seemingly irreparable version of what we longed for our lives to be. If this is you, I want you to know that I am praying for you as I work on these pages. I pray for you with a heart that may not know exactly what you are going through but that has also been broken by failure. I too have gazed around me in horror at the the damage I have caused others. And much to my dismay and grief and embarrassment, I still wound those I love.

Let me backtrack to what precipitated me to include these pages:

Our oldest granddaughter was getting married—a most wonderful and joyous occasion! We were thrilled for her and her husband-to-be, who we also love immensely. In addition to my normal load of housework, cooking, laundry, and caring for my young grandchildren, I was blessed but fatigued from helping prepare food for the reception.

Knowing I would be at the church all day on the Friday before the wedding, I had asked David more than a week in advance to run the errands that we usually handled together on Fridays, including grocery shopping, library pickup, and a stop for the local honey that helps with my allergies. I knew he would be going to Harrisonburg with our oldest son to pick up a long-awaited purchase, but I overheard him explain that the pickup would have to be after 12:30 because he had several errands to run. So I figured he had a plan and trusted him to handle it.

I got to church at 8:30 in the morning and returned home at 2:30 to shower and get ready for the rehearsal dinner. I looked for any groceries that needed to be put away but didn't see any. I also noticed that he had forgotten to take the library bag for the books I had on hold.

When he arrived home at about 4:00, he had no groceries, no

honey, and no books with him.

My initial response was unkind, accusing, and ugly. And then came the silence. For four miserable days (and I mean miserable for David *and* me), I would only interact with David when necessary, and even then, it was as little as possible. But while I was terse with my husband, I was quite long-winded with the Lord! He heard over and over again about David's failings and how *nothing* had changed in the forty-three years we had been married. How unfair and unkind he was. How I was simply never going to ask him or depend on him for anything ever again.

This was after reading the book *Unoffendable*, by Brant Hansen, not once, not twice, but *three* times; leading my small group through it as well; and watching a video course by Bruce Wilkenson on forgiveness! The Holy Spirit would nudge me about being unoffendable, about forgiving *everyone* for *everything*, and about Scriptures I have memorized that clearly expose not David's sin, but *my* own!

Can I be honest and say that I wanted to burn Brant's book? And while I complained to God, I avoided sitting *quietly* in His presence and being in His Word for those four days.

Finally, the guilt over my own behavior wore me down. The distance between me and David was uncomfortable, and knowing I was displeasing the Lord—again—was simply more than I could bear. I confessed to the Lord, I repented, and I apologized to David. I actually cried, not in anger and hurt but in sorrow over my unkindness, which was, to be honest, much worse than David's failure.

Even now, I am tempted to hide the truth: David *did* pick up the library books and the honey before the rehearsal dinner.

And he did get up early enough to go grocery shopping before the wedding on Saturday morning. But even then, I did not relent or climb down from my high seat of judgement.

After confessing, apologizing, and grieving my own failure, the Holy Spirit spoke to me: *"You have complained that in forty-three years, 'that'* [David's lack of follow-through] *has not changed. Do you see that in forty-three years 'this'* [my overreaction, retaliation, self-righteous indignation] *has not changed?"*

Now, the Holy Spirit is never cruel or condemning. It is hard to convey in writing, but His voice is quiet and gentle, and His correction is always under- and over-scored with much love and compassion. Along with this revelation that not merely stepped on but *crushed* my toes, He reminded me that I *have* changed.

In the past, I was so convinced of my own, dare I say, *perfection* (I can't think of another, less-cringy word) that I was deceived into believing my ugly, ungodly attitudes and actions were not wrong. This time, I was convicted, which means I am no longer deceived. Praise God for that! Also, although the incident lasted four too-long days, I would have drug it out for weeks in the past. This is a victory I can celebrate. I am improving!

Thank God for His mighty power at work within me. Here's to more of that and less of me.

There is a verse in the book of James that tells us to confess our sins to one another—not so that we can be forgiven, but so that we can be healed. To be *healed* of my pride and self-righteousness, I admitted my failure to two sisters in Christ. I was also healed of the guilt and shame I was still carrying as they gave tender affirmations of God's forgiveness and said that they could relate. We are all works in progress.

During our conversation, I commented that I had been exhausted from the wedding preparations. One dear sister said that someone had once shared this with her when she had made a similar excuse for wrong behavior: "If you only see the rats in your basement when you turn the lights on, it does not mean they are not there in the dark." In other words (mine, not hers), the unkindness and judgmentalism that I released cannot be blamed on fatigue. Sure, we are more vulnerable at such times. (Satan waited until Jesus was exhausted and starving before tempting Him in the wilderness.) But I am not to blame my circumstances for the way I act. I am to accept the responsibility for those rats in my basement that need to be eradicated. If I allow the Holy Spirit to help me get rid of them, they won't be there, whether the light is on or not.

Now, I realize that this little story is not an earth-shattering event, although I did deeply wound my dear husband's heart on a difficult day when he was missing Rebekah profoundly. But here's the thing: It reminded me in vivid, searing detail of the times I have responded in the same way to others' failures to do/say/be what I wanted/needed/expected. And with that reminder, I began to grieve again my much more devastating failures, with Davy and Rebekah in particular.

It was when revisiting that brutal pain that the Lord told me to write these chapters on having hope, not when our pain is due to tragedy, injustice, natural disaster, illness, loss, and so on, but when it's our own doing. Our own failure. Our own sin. Our own poor choices. Our own deception. Our own _____ (fill in the blank).

So where do we find hope when our greatest enemy stares

back at us in the bathroom mirror? Where do we find healing when we can barely stand ourselves? When we can hardly breathe under the weight of our sin, regrets, and possibly the condemnation and hatred of others? Where do we run for consolation when we know that we do not deserve anything other than the harshest condemnation and the greatest sentence a just God could dole out upon us?

The answer is the same as for any other time we are hopeless: to the arms of our loving God and the feet of Jesus.

Chapter 12
A Famous Fall from Grace

Let's look at a well-known example from the life of King David in the Bible. You may already be familiar with this story, but hang in here with me as I try to unpack it in a way that makes it applicable to you and me.

Second Samuel 11 begins, "In the spring, *at the time when kings go off to war, David sent Joab out with the king's men and the whole Israelite army.* They destroyed the Ammonites and besieged Rabbah. *But David remained in Jerusalem*" (NIV, emphasis mine).

This opening verse is important for context because it highlights what precipitated David's failures, which included adultery and murder. This story begins with David's failure to do what he was supposed to do and go where he was supposed to go.

An umbrella of protection covers us when we are walking in obedience to God. *But* obedience to God and love for God do not mean we will never have trials or troubles or deep loss/grief. With that being said, there are certain protections we enjoy when we are obedient that are given up when we are not. For example, if a husband and wife do not have sex with other people, they are at zero risk for a sexually transmitted infection. (However, this protection requires fidelity on both sides! A faithful wife or husband can be exposed to and acquire an STI if their spouse cheats.)

Let's continue our story:

> One evening David got up from his bed and walked around on the roof of the palace. From the roof he saw a woman bathing. The woman was very beautiful, and *David sent someone to find out about her*. The man said, "She is Bathsheba, the daughter of Eliam and the wife of Uriah the Hittite. *Then* David sent messengers to get her. She came to him, and he slept with her.

In a place where he should not have been, David saw something he should not have seen. Instead of quickly removing himself from the temptation, he sought out more information. And even when this information revealed that the woman he was lusting after was taken, David still followed through on his desire to have her. David could not claim innocence or ignorance. He knew what he was doing was wrong.

Did this occur only once? Was Bathsheba willing, or was she raped? (David was the king, after all. She may not have been allowed to turn him down.) We do not know the answers to these questions. But we do know this: David willingly committed adultery. He abused his power and gravely sinned against another human being. I have a feeling that he thought he could get away with this "slip-up" and no one (who mattered or could do anything about it) would ever find out.

Then comes the shocking revelation: "The woman conceived and sent word to David, saying, 'I am pregnant.'" So much for no one knowing! Having committed a grievous sin, David now devises a plan to cover up his wrongdoing:

So David sent this word to Joab: "Send me Uriah the Hittite." And Joab sent him to David. When Uriah came to him, David asked him how Joab was, how the soldiers were and how the war was going. Then David said to Uriah, "Go down to your house and wash your feet." So Uriah left the palace, and a gift from the king was sent after him. But Uriah slept at the entrance to the palace with all his master's servants and did not go down to his house.

David was told, "Uriah did not go home." So he asked Uriah, "Haven't you just come from a military campaign? Why didn't you go home?"

Uriah said to David, "The ark and Israel and Judah are staying in tents, and my commander Joab and my lord's men are camped in the open country. How could I go to my house to eat and drink and make love to my wife? As surely as you live, I will not do such a thing!"

Then David said to him, "Stay here one more day, and tomorrow I will send you back." So Uriah remained in Jerusalem that day and the next. At David's invitation, he ate and drank with him, and David made him drunk. But in the evening Uriah went out to sleep on his mat among his master's servants; he did not go home.

David's Plan: Send Bathsheba's husband home, where he would most certainly take advantage of the opportunity to sleep with his wife after being away at war. Thus, when Bathsheba's pregnancy was revealed, everyone would assume the baby was Uriah's. Simple! A sure thing. And quite devious.

The Problem: Uriah was a good, honorable man. He refused to take advantage of the situation when his fellow warriors were risking their lives on the battlefield. Even when David tried to get him drunk enough to set aside his convictions,

Uriah remained the man of integrity that he was.

Plan #1 backfired. Now what?

> In the morning David wrote a letter to Joab and sent it with Uriah. In it he wrote, "Put Uriah out in front where the fighting is fiercest. Then withdraw from him so he will be struck down and die."
>
> So while Joab had the city under siege, he put Uriah at a place where he knew the strongest defenders were. When the men of the city came out and fought against Joab, some of the men in David's army fell; moreover, Uriah the Hittite died.

Instead of simply coming clean, David progresses from adultery to murder. Oh, that we could all learn the truth that the more we try to cover up our sin, the further we sink into the mire of a corrupted heart and the more damage we inflict on others and our own souls!

At this point, we should remember that this is a true story about King David. God's anointed king. "A man after God's own heart." A man who, from childhood, knew, loved, and followed God. Who depended on God and trusted Him in the darkest of circumstances. Surely, upon the news of the death of an innocent man, whose blood was on his hands, David would break down in sorrow and repentance.

> Joab sent David a full account of the battle. He instructed the messenger: "When you have finished giving the king this account of the battle, the king's anger may flare up, and he may ask you, 'Why did you get so close to the city to fight? Didn't you know they would shoot arrows from the wall? Who killed Abimelek son of Jerub-Besheth? Didn't a woman drop an upper millstone on him from the wall, so that he died in Thebez? Why did you get so close to the wall?' If he asks you this, then say to him,

'Moreover, your servant Uriah the Hittite is dead.'"

The messenger set out, and when he arrived he told David everything Joab had sent him to say. The messenger said to David, "The men overpowered us and came out against us in the open, but we drove them back to the entrance of the city gate. Then the archers shot arrows at your servants from the wall, and some of the king's men died. Moreover, your servant Uriah the Hittite is dead."

David told the messenger, "Say this to Joab: 'Don't let this upset you; the sword devours one as well as another. Press the attack against the city and destroy it.' Say this to encourage Joab."

What?! "Say this to Joab: 'Don't let this upset you; the sword devours one as well as another.'" No sorrow over the loss of Uriah's life. No ownership or repentance. No care or concern for the grief this would bring Bathsheba (for she did indeed grieve, according to 2 Samuel 11:26).

With no regard for anyone but himself, David simply waited until the "proper" time of mourning was over and then brought Bathsheba into his home, along with his six other wives and concubines. I can't help but wonder about Bathsheba's frame of mind at this point. But David? He's still king. He's still in charge. No one dares make any accusations: *Hasn't he made it right by marrying the woman in the end? Isn't this what all kings do anyway? After all, he got another male child out of the deal.*

I do not know what David was thinking or feeling, but verse 27 reveals the feelings of the Lord God: "But the thing David had done displeased the LORD."

David may have fooled the majority of his kingdom. He may have been so powerful that those who knew what he had done did not dare speak against him. He may have felt that it was a done deal and that he had gotten off scot-free. But the solemn truth is that no one ever escapes the consequences of their sin. Those consequences may never come to light visibly, but the damage done to our souls is graphic and explicit in the spirit realm. And we will all have to stand before God one day.

Please do not think that I am pointing at anyone other than myself. I take it very seriously and with a hefty dose of trepidation that God has seen every failure of mine, and that one day I will give an account for all of them. I praise God that I will not suffer punishment from Him because Jesus took it for me (and for *you*, if you are a Christ-follower). Hallelujah! But I still do not look forward to standing before the Lord with my sin exposed.

Back to the story of David. He did not have to wait until heaven to address his sin. Nathan was a prophet of God, who spoke for God to the people . . . and even to the king. Our story resumes at 2 Samuel 12:1–6:

> The LORD sent Nathan to David. When he came to him, he said, "There were two men in a certain town, one rich and the other poor. The rich man had a very large number of sheep and cattle, but the poor man had nothing except one little ewe lamb he had bought. He raised it, and it grew up with him and his children. It shared his food, drank from his cup and even slept in his arms. It was like a daughter to him.
>
> "Now a traveler came to the rich man, but the rich man refrained from taking one of his own sheep or cattle to prepare a meal for the traveler who had come to him. Instead, he took the ewe lamb that belonged to the poor man and prepared it for the one who had come to him."
>
> David burned with anger against the man and said to Nathan, "As surely as the LORD lives, the man who did this must die! He

must pay for that lamb four times over, because he did such a
thing and had no pity."

Dear ones, how quick we are to recognize and condemn and demand justice for the sins of others, when we can be so blind to our own. Unaware that Nathan was concocting a made-up story, David thought he was sharing an actual crime within his kingdom. Rage, righteous anger, and a desire to make this evil man pay rose up in him. I also believe a deep compassion and sorrow for the poor man's loss moved David's emotions.

And then, with surgical precision, Nathan drops the bomb of irrefutable clarity and truth: "Then Nathan said to David, 'You are the man!'"

I picture David falling to his knees in sorrow, shame, and horror as the realization of what he has done, how far he has fallen, and God knowing it all reverberates throughout his entire being. The shock waves must have rocked him. But Nathan wasn't yet finished with the indictment David thought he had so skillfully avoided.

> This is what the LORD, the God of Israel, says: "I anointed you king over Israel, and I delivered you from the hand of Saul. I gave your master's house to you, and your master's wives into your arms. I gave you all Israel and Judah. And if all this had been too little, I would have given you even more. Why did you despise the word of the LORD by doing what is evil in his eyes? You struck down Uriah the Hittite with the sword and took his wife to be your own. You killed him with the sword of the Ammonites. Now, therefore, the sword will never depart from your house, because you despised me and took the wife of Uriah the Hittite to be your own."

> This is what the LORD says: "Out of your own household I am going to bring calamity on you. Before your very eyes I will take

your wives and give them to one who is close to you, and he will sleep with your wives in broad daylight. You did it in secret, but I will do this thing in broad daylight before all Israel."

Pause for a moment and reread that last paragraph. Would this not seem like a burden too heavy to bear, no matter how deserved it was? Have you been there? Feeling like you will most certainly be crushed under your guilt, shame, and regret? I can tell you honestly that I have, but surely the reality that this man—beloved of God, the very king God chose to rule and lead His people—can relate to your pain carries much more weight.

David replies to Nathan with humility and, I believe, visible anguish—tears running down his face, slumped over, far removed from the usual upright posture and dignified demeanor of a king. "I have sinned against the LORD," he said.

We breathe a deep sigh of relief! David repents. God will forgive him. All will be well. But brace yourself because Nathan is not yet finished relaying the word of the Lord to David. He continues: "The LORD has taken away your sin. You are not going to die. But because by doing this you have shown utter contempt for the LORD, the son born to you will die."

What? Wait! Because David sinned, an innocent baby died? Bathsheba not only has to mourn the death of her first husband but also her precious child? I can hear you now: "Nancy *Jo*! I thought this was supposed to give me hope?"

Please don't give up yet! Our story is hard, but it is not yet finished.

> After Nathan had gone home, the LORD struck the child that Uriah's wife had borne to David, and he became ill. David

pleaded with God for the child. He fasted and spent the nights lying in sackcloth on the ground. The elders of his household stood beside him to get him up from the ground, but he refused, and he would not eat any food with them.

On the seventh day the child died. David's attendants were afraid to tell him that the child was dead, for they thought, "While the child was still living, he wouldn't listen to us when we spoke to him. How can we now tell him the child is dead? He may do something desperate."

David noticed that his attendants were whispering among themselves, and he realized the child was dead. "Is the child dead?" he asked.

"Yes," they replied, "he is dead."

Then David got up from the ground. After he had washed, put on lotions and changed his clothes, he went into the house of the LORD and worshiped. Then he went to his own house, and at his request they served him food, and he ate.

His attendants asked him, "Why are you acting this way? While the child was alive, you fasted and wept, but now that the child is dead, you get up and eat!"

He answered, "While the child was still alive, I fasted and wept. I thought, 'Who knows? The LORD may be gracious to me and let the child live.' But now that he is dead, why should I go on fasting? Can I bring him back again? I will go to him, but he will not return to me."

"He went to the house of the Lord and worshiped. . . ."

First, let's examine David's attitude and actions. No longer is he a demanding king, manipulating everyone and everything with no regard to the feelings or very lives of others. No longer is he proud, dishing out commands or dictates of how others should feel. He is simply a man. A broken, contrite, and grieved human being. Truly filled with sorrow for what he has done and how his choices have harmed other people. Now, instead of barking orders to his subjects, he is pleading with the King of kings. Not for himself, mind you, but for his child and for his wife Bathsheba.

And what was the result? His precious baby still died. Bathsheba was not spared the additional grief. His repentance did not buy him anything, it seems.

But did you see it? That tiny flicker of hope? "Now that he is dead, why should I go on fasting? Can I bring him back again? I will go to him, but he will not return to me." *This* is the concrete evidence of David's changed heart. After repenting and pleading for a different outcome, even in the face of God's silence, which could be translated as a cold, distant, vengeful *"No!"* David chose to fall back on what he knew: God is good. God is holy. God is with him and for him. God is worthy of all glory and honor and praise, even when He does not remove the consequences of our sin. David's hope was in his good, good Father *and* the promise of heaven: being reunited with his precious little boy one day.

There is one more brief chapter in this particular story (although in the story of God's redemption for all mankind, the story continues to this day and beyond): "Then David comforted his wife Bathsheba, and he went to her and made love to her. She gave birth to a son, and they named him Solomon."

David and Bathsheba's relationship began with abuse, adultery, murder, and possibly rape. But it ended with David being a caring husband who comforted his wife. Surely that comfort included owning his wrongs against her and Uriah. Surely it included a broken heart for the pain he had caused her. I say this not just from wishful thinking but because the Hebrew word for *comforted* can be defined in the following ways: "to be sorry," "to pity/console," and "to repent."

And Solomon? Although not the firstborn, or second, or third, Solomon became the next king of Israel. He is considered the wisest and richest king to ever rule on earth.

Here is where we will end the story of David's great personal failure and turn to what we can learn and apply to our own.

Chapter 13
Out of Hopelessness

Let's begin by setting one thing in stone: Any personal failure is ours and ours alone. James tells us that God is never tempted to do wrong, and He never tempts anyone else. And while others may tempt us, place us in difficult situations, betray us, harm us, lie about us, cheat us, deny us what is rightfully ours, and spitefully use us, we must own our wrongdoing.

The Lord just "smacked me upside the head" with something I hate to admit, but it applies perfectly to the point I am trying to make. Let me start by saying, I married an imperfect man. I know. *Gasp! Shock! Horror!*

There have been times when he was unkind, when he failed to do what he should and did what he should not. In other words, he is no different than me or any other human being.

Now, my nature is one that avoids confrontation like the plague. (I am doing better by God's grace and coming to understand that avoiding confrontation never fixes anything.) During the first years of our marriage, instead of addressing conflicts as they occurred—even small conflicts but especially big ones—I would bury them. I didn't bury them too deep, though; I had to be able to dig them up, polish them up, and use them to feed my resentment and fuel my anger. Eventually, when they amassed to a huge pile of volatile lava, I used them to excuse my eruptions of anger and brutal remarks.

I would fly off the handle, uncovering (and probably embellishing) every offense David had committed, which I had not addressed when I could do so in a calm manner. I would cry, yes, but they were tears of anger rather than hurt—perhaps hurt that turned into anger as it simmered within my soul.

Then, after lengthy periods of silence, I would know I needed to apologize. (Is this sounding familiar?) The problem was that my apology always hinged on what *he* did wrong. If only he had or hadn't done this or that, I wouldn't have responded the way I did. So I *was* wrong, but it was still really *his* fault that I was wrong. Get it?

1. Ownership

The first step in finding freedom, healing, and forgiveness from our failure, as counterproductive as it sounds, is owning our failure. Admitting our failure. Taking full responsibility for what we did wrong, apart from placing blame on anyone else or any situation we found ourselves in.

Note King David's exact words upon hearing that the man who stole the pet lamb and slaughtered it for his dinner was actually himself: "I have sinned against the Lord."

I have done wrong. There is no one else to blame. I have no excuse. I am the one who chose to sin. And in my sin, I sinned against the Almighty, the holy God of the universe. Even if I hurt no other person. Even if I was never "found out." Even if I justified and excused my actions until the day I died. I sinned against God Himself.

Ownership is the first step on a rough path that eventually leads to a very beautiful, peaceful, joyous place.

This goes along with our earlier conversation about the need to confess to others, not only to be healed but also to escape the power we give the enemy when we hide our failures. God desires to rush in and forgive. To comfort. To redeem. To correct and teach in order to strengthen. To do what a *good* father does when a child disobeys. But His hands are tied until we come to humbly admit what we have done and accept responsibility for our failure.

When we reach this point, Satan loses all power over that failure. God is able to step in and do the miraculous: sustain us, strengthen us, and bring redemption—to use our failure to both transform us more into the image of God and be a place from which we can minister to others.

Have you, dear one, owned your failure? Can you humble yourself to the point of not blaming parents, friends, significant others, bosses, co-workers, the government . . . God? Can you say what you did wrong and, with utter sincerity, confess, "God, I have sinned against You and _____"? (There are most likely others you can include in that confession.)

2. Honesty

Step two on our path to hope and light after owning our failure is to be honest about it. I don't mean you need to purchase a billboard and post your failures on it for all to see. I mean, rather than trying to cover up your missteps, rather than seeking to camouflage your wrongs, you open up to anyone you have harmed and, if possible, give restitution.

I think of the ladies I ministered to in jail. They showed such sorrow over their mistakes, and they were honest about them in class. But when preparing to go before a judge, they would often ask me if it was okay to lie because if they didn't, the outcome could be severe. Maybe you too are in a situation in which if you were to come totally clean, you could lose your job, your reputation, your position of influence, your dignity.

There are Scriptures that apply specifically to such situations. Before we get to them, I want to say that many, many verses in the Bible speak of fearing the Lord. Please consider studying them. But I want to clarify that when the Bible tells us to "fear God," it does not mean to be terrified of what He might do to us. It is speaking of a deep reverence and respect born out of an understanding that God is our good, good Father *and* He is also Almighty God—holy, righteous, and perfectly just.

When we find ourselves wondering if we should lie or shade the truth or be "slightly deceitful" for whatever reason, we need to recognize what is at the root of that line of reasoning: a fear of man and a lack of fear of God. Look at this tiny sampling of verses:

Proverbs 29:25: "Fearing people is a dangerous trap, but trusting the LORD means safety."

Deuteronomy 8:6: "So obey the commands of the LORD your God by walking in his ways and fearing him." (NKJV: "Therefore you shall keep the commandments of the LORD your God, to walk in His ways and to fear Him.")

Luke 1:50: "He shows mercy from generation to generation to all who fear him."

Psalm 112:1: "Praise the LORD! How joyful are those who fear the LORD and delight in obeying his commands."

For those dear ladies who struggled with whether to be honest in court, I would ask them: "Do you want God's blessing? Do you want God's mercy? If so, then you must be honest." It is that simple *and* that difficult. It is always hard to choose the unseen promises for *future* mercy and blessings over the scary scenarios of *present* consequences if we choose to uncover ourselves rather than risk being uncovered by someone else or by God. Again, there's that futile hope that we can hide our wrongdoing.

Just this past year, a well-known pastor of a megachurch was found out for sins decades old. This pastor had shared such excellent teachings, and I actually learned a lot from him through his video lessons and books. Without getting bogged down in details, he admitted *this* sin, this personal moral failure, that he had committed long ago. He seemingly repented. (I say *seemingly* not in judgment but in the acknowledgment that I do not know his heart.) I do believe that he did not fall back into that sin again.

But here is the problem that has destroyed his ministry, brought tremendous harm to the Body of Christ, and, I imagine, caused deep hurt to his family: While he confessed and owned *this* sin, he concealed *that* sin. When the full truth came out, irreparable damage was done to his reputation and his ministry.

What would have happened had he been completely upfront to begin with? Maybe he would have never become the well-known figure he was. Maybe he would have never tasted the sweetness of leading such a big church, of publishing so many books and videos, and of meeting so many well-known people. Maybe he would have never been in the spotlight. But I think if he could go back now, he would have chosen a life of obscurity over where this choice to be less than 100-percent honest has led him. I certainly hope he would! Otherwise, there has been no true repentance.

God's ways are not easy: Love your neighbor. Bless those who persecute you. Get rid of all anger. Forgive anyone who offends you. Die to self—wait, do *what* to self? Anyone who says these commands are easy to keep is living outside of reality! But God's ways are always, always, *always* best for us.

Obedience to God always pays off in the long run—if not here on earth, then for all eternity in heaven, where God promises to reward us for our obedience. (Although I believe with all my heart that obedience does pay off here on earth, sometimes it takes a while for that mercy and those blessings to become evident to us. And sometimes we forfeit them by losing faith and falling back into sin or compromise.)

So we must own our failure and sin. We must be honest about our failure and sin and not try to hide or partially confess, even in order to avoid harsh consequences.

3. Acceptance

The next step on our path toward hope is a very difficult one, one we can be standing on one moment and then fall off the next and have to climb back on. We accept the consequences of our failures. Exactly what do I mean by that? I mean that when I abuse someone's trust and they do not trust me anymore, I do not accuse them of not forgiving me or being unfair. I acknowledge the reason they do not trust me, and that reason is 100 percent on me.

We can see this acceptance clearly in David's response to Nathan's calling out of his poor choices and sin. David did not argue with or defend himself to Nathan. David did not cry out that God was unfair in the loss of his little son, nor did he try to bargain with Him. "O God, if You will just spare the life of my son, I promise I will _____." David accepted the consequences, even as he prayed that God might relent. And when that prayer went unanswered, he still chose to worship God.

When I do something wrong that lands me in a place I do not like—jail, separated from my spouse or other loved ones, a hospital bed, fired—I do not complain about unfairness or other people and accuse others (or God) of having it out for me. I accept that I am where I am because of the choices I made.

There was a man who was driving a motorcycle over 100 miles per hour when he came up on a very sharp curve. He was injured, although not terribly, by the grace of God. But his motorcycle was totaled. His response: "God does not like me. He has it out for me."

While it is easy for you and me (unless you happen to be a hotrod motorcyclist) to see the blatant error in his thinking, can we be humble enough to look at our own lives and see where we have disowned responsibility for our actions?

I loved ministering in the jail. I adored those ladies! I still love on the ones I am in contact with. I desperately longed for those beautiful, gifted, dear women to serve their time and go on to live lives of freedom in Christ, being productive in their communities as well as reunited with family. Some did—praise the Lord—and I am so happy for them! Some did not, and for them, I grieve. As the years passed, I became better and better at guessing which ones I would unfortunately be seeing again in the jail. Are you ready for this?

The women who were honest about their crime, whatever it was, and who saw their time in jail as a just consequence—one that they did not like but accepted as the result of their poor choices—and used the time to better themselves (Bible study, classes, work release, etc.) were the ones less likely to return to jail. They are the ones who now have excellent jobs—in some cases, managers of their places of business. They are the ones who are now able to be caring mothers and grandmothers. They are the ones who are truly living life! They have decided that whatever it was that landed them in jail is not worth the (just/fair) consequences they would have to pay.

When ministering to married couples who had experienced a break in trust, I would always try to help the person at fault understand that no matter how frustrating or unfounded the continued lack of trust was, no matter how honest/faithful/trustworthy they had been since then, the lack of trust was not their spouse's fault. The blame rested on the one who broke the trust, as did the responsibility to work—hard and over time—to earn that trust back.

And here is the crazy part: When the person who broke trust is willing to address the lack of trust, they are the ones who end up in strong, loving marriages. They say something like, "I realize you do not trust me, and that is my fault. I want very much to earn your trust back, and I will be completely open and willing to let you examine and confirm whatever you need to for as long as it takes to earn your trust again."[4]

4. Letting Go of Expectations

This is perhaps the most difficult step on our path. We must

---

4. I am not condoning someone who holds a failure over another's head and badgers them about it for years. I realize there are people like that, and they are equally as wrong.

free others from any expectations of forgiveness or restoration of the relationship.

Please notice that I specifically used the word *expectations*. That does not mean that we cannot pray for, hope for, long for restoration, but we must not expect and certainly not demand.

When people fail to forgive us, refuse to believe we have changed, continue to label us in derogatory ways, speak unkindly about us, be ever grateful for those who do rally around us! Thank them and thank God for them. Even if there is not a single person who fills this gap, we must believe God when He says that we are forgiven, we are loved, we are treasured, and He is able to redeem even our worst failures.

Run to Jesus with the hurts of rejection, ridicule, and unjust treatment. He understands better than any human ever could, and unlike us, He is completely undeserving of anything negative said about Him, much less the beyond-horrific treatment He received when He lived here on earth.

Chapter 14

Lament

You may have noticed that our journey toward hope after personal failure includes a lot of attitude choices. The four steps again are as follows:

1. Own and take responsibility for failure, refusing to blame anyone else or excuse or lighten the severity.
2. Be honest about the whole truth. Trust that God will be free to bless and help in ways He is not when we are in any way deceitful.
3. Accept the consequences of failure, whatever those may look like. Do not fight them. Pray, asking God to use the consequences to make you more like Jesus and help you learn from your mistakes.
4. Do not place expectations on people to forgive, be reunited, believe, or trust you. Rest in the knowledge that God knows your heart, and ask the Holy Spirit to help that be enough.

We are going to look at King David again, but first, I would like to point you to one of the most powerful true stories of someone who walked out those steps: Karla Faye Tucker. In the book, *Karla Faye Tucker Set Free*, written by Linda Strom who knew Karla well, Karla's story of salvation, redemption, and transformation is powerfully laid out. Convicted of the brutal slaying of two people with a pickaxe, Karla was given the death sentence and was the first woman to be executed in Texas since the 1800s. I highly recommend this book as a modern-day example of what it looks like to be forgiven for the most heinous of crimes and set free to be loved by God. Karla's final words before being executed still ring in my ears. You will be inspired and challenged and find a very unexpected role model in Karla Faye Tucker.

I want to peek back at the steps above before we move on. Throughout this process, I believe we must also suffer a period of grief. I have a feeling that most of us have had an "I'm sorry" offered us, without any true remorse from someone who hurt us. I do not believe God wants us to remain in tortured remorse over our failings, no matter how dreadful. But I do believe His Word tells us that if we are truly repentant (that is, we own, recognize, and desire with all our heart to turn from our sin and be obedient to God in the future), sorrow will be a part of that process. Let's look at a few verses:

2 Corinthians 7:10: "For the kind of sorrow God wants us to experience leads us away from sin and results in salvation. There's no regret for that kind of sorrow. But worldly sorrow, which lacks repentance, results in spiritual death."

James 4:9: "Let there be tears for what you have done. Let there be sorrow and deep grief. Let there be sadness instead of laughter, and gloom instead of joy."

Luke 18:9–14:

> Then Jesus told this story to some who had great confidence in their own righteousness and scorned everyone else: "Two men

went to the Temple to pray. One was a Pharisee, and the other was a despised tax collector. The Pharisee stood by himself and prayed this prayer: 'I thank you, God, that I am not like other people—cheaters, sinners, adulterers. I'm certainly not like that tax collector! I fast twice a week, and I give you a tenth of my income.'

"But the tax collector stood at a distance and dared not even lift his eyes to heaven as he prayed. Instead, he beat his chest in sorrow, saying, 'O God, be merciful to me, for I am a sinner.' I tell you, this sinner, not the Pharisee, returned home justified before God. For those who exalt themselves will be humbled, and those who humble themselves will be exalted."

If you and I do not genuinely grieve our failures and the harm we cause ourselves and others, as well as the hurt we cause the heart of God, I believe we are not truly sorry. We should long with all our hearts to alleviate pain and do things differently in the future.

Some of us do a lot of lamenting: over the consequences, how it has cost or inconvenienced us, over the "failure" of others to let us off the hook or reinstate us in some way. But sorrow over circumstances is what 2 Corinthians refers to as "worldly sorrow." This sorrow produces a lot of tears and bitterness, but nothing of value and certainly not a changed heart.

God does not want us to stay in this place of mourning our failures. James 4:10 goes on to say, "Humble yourselves before the Lord, and he will lift you up in honor." We must go through the four steps with genuine sorrow and excruciatingly honest humility. And when we do, oh, our loving Father will lift us up in honor! God will see our hearts, even if no one else does. God will set us free, even if we are behind bars. We will experience a joyous freedom we may never have known before!

But here's where I want to delve a little deeper—maybe a lot deeper. Those of us who cause great harm to others, intentionally or unintentionally, get stuck in a pit of grief, shame, and regret so deep and so dark that even the tiniest glimmers of hope have a hard time penetrating. I know this because I have lived in that pit. I have suffered that crushing weight. I have felt void of the hope that I could ever rise up again into the light of joy.

I have shared before that when my grief counselor asked me about three years after Rebekah's death what was the hardest part of grief, I told her it was all my regrets. The song "How He Loves" by David Crowder Band was new in 2009. I remember sitting and listening to the lyrics, "Oh, how He loves us," and just weeping because *how* could God love me after all my failures? How? The song contains a huge part of the answer: His mercy! His grace! His genuine affection for me! What is it that causes us to doubt God's love, forgiveness, mercy, and ability to redeem after our greatest failures?

The simple answer, I believe, is our inability to love like God loves. We cannot fathom the kind of love that sees past failures, mistakes, horrific sins and, rather than being repelled, is drawn closer. No human being has ever modeled that kind of love in the face of grand disgrace to the extent that it exists in God, other than Jesus, who, although completely human, was also completely God.

Perhaps you grew up like me, with wonderful, loving parents who loved God and were genuinely good. Although this is true, I can clearly remember my mom telling me, "God is disappointed in you," when I did something wrong. And having grown up this way, what did I tell my children? You guessed it!

I grew up thinking that my sin distanced God from me. My

failures somehow affected His love for me. Not that He stopped loving me, but that He didn't love me quite as much. That His anger over my sin would somehow eclipse the affection the song describes.

These were my thoughts as a child after committing little acts of disobedience, telling a lie, being unkind—the list is endless. So what was I to think when I came face to face with my failures as a parent? I would find myself wondering if I had not committed these failures, would my daughter still be alive? Unkind words and actions that I will never be able to apologize for. Things I would have given my right arm to be able to go back and do or re-do to show Rebekah how very, very much I did love her! Even writing those words caused my eyes to fill with tears, and I find myself now just so, so sorry and broken.

We are going to look at David's beautiful psalm, written after Nathan confronted him about his sin with Bathsheba, the murder of Uriah, and the loss of his baby boy.

Psalm 51

> *For the choir director: A psalm of David, regarding the time Nathan the prophet came to him after David had committed adultery with Bathsheba.*

> Have mercy on me, O God,
> because of your unfailing love.
> Because of your great compassion,
> blot out the stain of my sins.
> Wash me clean from my guilt.
> Purify me from my sin.
> For I recognize my rebellion;
> it haunts me day and night.
> Against you, and you alone, have I sinned;
> I have done what is evil in your sight.

You will be proved right in what you say,
and your judgment against me is just.
For I was born a sinner—
yes, from the moment my mother conceived me
But you desire honesty from the womb,
teaching me wisdom even there.
Purify me from my sins, and I will be clean;
wash me, and I will be whiter than snow.
Oh, give me back my joy again;
you have broken me—
now let me rejoice.
Don't keep looking at my sins.
Remove the stain of my guilt.
Create in me a clean heart, O God.
Renew a loyal spirit within me.
Do not banish me from your presence,
and don't take your Holy Spirit from me.
Restore to me the joy of your salvation,
and make me willing to obey you.
Then I will teach your ways to rebels,
and they will return to you.
Forgive me for shedding blood, O God who saves;
then I will joyfully sing of your forgiveness.
Unseal my lips, O LORD,
that my mouth may praise you.
You do not desire a sacrifice, or I would offer one.
You do not want a burnt offering.
The sacrifice you desire is a broken spirit.
You will not reject a broken and repentant heart, O God.
Look with favor on Zion and help her;
rebuild the walls of Jerusalem.
Then you will be pleased with sacrifices offered in the
    right spirit—
with burnt offerings and whole burnt offerings.
Then bulls will again be sacrificed on your altar.

Chapter 15
Grace After Grief

It would be easy for anyone perusing my shelves to spot the books that impact me the most. They are underlined, highlighted, asterisked, circled, and notated. My Bible is no different, and I would like to encourage you to take the time to slowly meditate on the psalm on the previous pages, either here or in your Bible, marking, highlighting, underlining, and writing questions and applications or thanks and praise in the margins.

Perhaps in a journal, record what Psalm 51 reveals about God's love and mercy. Where do you see David implementing the steps we have talked about? What about God's ability to do the impossible in and for us, even after our failures?

Now, let's look at some other scriptures that address some of David's requests.

Isaiah 1:18:

> "Come now, let's settle this,"
> says the Lord.
> "Though your sins are like scarlet,
> I will make them as white as snow.

> Though they are red like crimson,
> I will make them as white as wool."

Lamentations 3:21–23:

> Yet I still dare to hope
> when I remember this:
> The faithful love of the LORD never ends!
> His mercies never cease.
> Great is his faithfulness;
> his mercies begin afresh each morning.

Titus 3:4–5:

> When God our Savior revealed his kindness and love, he saved us, not because of the righteous things we had done, but because of his mercy. He washed away our sins, giving us a new birth and new life through the Holy Spirit.

One of my favorites is Hebrews 4:16 (ESV): "Let us then with confidence draw near to the throne of grace, that we may receive mercy and find grace to help in time of need." (For when do we need mercy the most? After failure, of course!)

Hebrews 10:10 (NLV): "Our sins are washed away and we are made clean because Christ gave His own body as a gift to God. He did this once for all time."

Romans 12:1–2 (NIV):

> Therefore, I urge you, brothers and sisters, in view of God's mercy, to offer your bodies as a living sacrifice, holy and pleasing to God—this is your true and proper worship. Do not conform to the pattern of this world, but be transformed by the renewing of your mind. Then you will be able to test and approve what God's will is—his good, pleasing and perfect will.

Hebrews 13:5: "Don't love money; be satisfied with what you have. For God has said, 'I will never fail you. I will never abandon you.'"

In order to have confident hope, we have to believe God when He tells us we are forgiven. We have to believe God when His Word tells us that *nothing* in all creation will ever be able to separate us from His love. We must believe God when He says He can redeem all things for our good. He does not say, "All things, except if you mess up really, really badly!"

This, dear friend, is what I was so desperate to understand. I knew God's grace was amazing. I knew His grace was powerful enough to save the worst sinners of all time. What I did not fully grasp was the truth that I never need God's grace less than I did the moment He saved me. Once saved, it is not up to me to get my act together or suffer God's wrath. Jesus died for my sins: past, present, and future. If you know Jesus as your Lord and Savior, the same is true for you! Jesus suffered God's wrath. He endured the just punishment for our sins (death and hell). God is not angry with us when we fail. He is not frustrated. He is not disappointed. And He is not ashamed of us. Our behavior might bring shame to His name, but He is never ashamed of *us*.

I want to share three different writings from three different authors about this. (Two in this chapter, and one in a later chapter.) We will begin with one of the devotions from Sara Young's *Dear Jesus*:

> Beloved, it is utterly impossible for Me to stop loving you. Your relationship with Me is so saturated in grace that the two are forever inseparable. Meat that has been marinated in a sauce cannot become unmarinated. The longer it soaks, the deeper the marinade penetrates, flavoring and tenderizing the meat. You

have been soaking in grace ever since I became your Savior. The longer you "marinate," the more fully My grace permeates our relationship. It is impossible for you to become un-graced!

I want you to rest in the perfection of your salvation. My glorious grace makes you holy and blameless in My sight. So, nothing you do or fail to do could ever separate you from My Love.

Then Sarah shares these scriptures:

Ephesians 2:8 (NKJV): "For by grace you have been saved through faith. . ."

Romans 8:38–39 (NIV): "For I am convinced that neither death nor life, neither angels nor demons, neither the present nor the future, nor any powers, neither height nor depth, nor anything else in all creation, will be able to separate us from the love of God that is in Christ Jesus our Lord."

Isaiah 61:10 (NIV): "I delight greatly in the LORD; my soul rejoices in my God. For he has clothed me with garments of salvation and arrayed me in a robe of righteousness."

Ephesians 1:4–6:

> Even before he made the world, God loved us and chose us in Christ to be holy and without fault in his eyes. God decided in advance to adopt us into his own family by bringing us to himself through Jesus Christ. This is what he wanted to do, and it gave him great pleasure. So we praise God for the glorious grace he has poured out on us who belong to his dear Son.[5]

---

5. Please note that this is the New Living Translation, while in the book, Sarah uses the NIV again.

Let's flow from this poignant capture of God's heart for us to a passage from the book *Unoffendable* by Brant Hansen:

> But here's a bigger problem, and it's based on years of interacting with thousands of self-described Christians: It's not merely that we're not attentive to the fact that God loves us. I suspect many of us actually just don't believe it.

Brant goes on to state his evidence: because we act like God is displeased with us. Then he challenges his readers to take the following test:

> **What does a properly religious leader do when seeing his so-called best friends for the first time after they disowned him and betrayed him in his hour of need?**
>
> **a.** Show them the error of their wicked ways by pronouncing harsh, deserved judgment upon them.
> **b.** Give them a stern talking-to, but offer forgiveness if they prove themselves truly penitent.
> **c.** Fry 'em up a hearty breakfast.

Jesus chose c.

> And the breakfast didn't even come with a good scolding or an ironic, "Hey, nice job, fellas. Appreciate the way you handled that with such class." He just wanted to be with them again. This was after He had been mocked, beaten, and murdered...

> You suspect you're unlovable? He loves you. You wonder, deep down, if anyone could really, truly know you and still want you? He knows you better than you know you. And He wants you.

> You've given up on yourself? He hasn't given up on you. This isn't feel-good talk; it's the rightful conclusion we can draw from the cross itself.

He still loves us because He's a Father . . . the One we've always wanted.

When we fail, when our choices are disastrous, what is Jesus's response? He wants to be with us, to love on us, to bless us, to enjoy us. Moreover, if we allow Him to work in us, He can bring healing and restoration out of whatever harm we have done, for our good and His glory.

Are you thinking back to our story about David and scratching your head? We read in 2 Samuel 12:14 (NIV), "But because by doing this you have shown utter contempt for the LORD, the son born to you will die."

Do you believe that this verse (and others like it) contradicts everything Sarah Young, Brant Hansen, and I have shared with you? Hang with me if you do!

First, I admit that I am no theologian. What I am sharing is from my heart, but it is also based on studying the Bible for many years, sitting under the biblically sound teachings of numerous pastors, and reading the works of those who *are* theologians. I also have experienced the goodness, grace, and mercy of God in my own life, which has been filled with failures!

This is what I believe: All the punishment for sin was placed upon Jesus when He died on the cross. (See Romans 3:25, 2 Corinthians 5:21, etc.). God is completely just and fair, and therefore, to punish us as well as punishing Jesus would be a breach of justice. Even in our very broken justice system, we are protected from double jeopardy.

What we suffer because of our sins (and the sins of others) is the *consequence* of sin. Think back to that man on the motorcycle. God did not push his motorcycle over to punish him.

God did not desire for him to suffer physical pain or the loss of property. The man's choice to excessively exceed the speed limit around a sharp curve had the natural consequence of human injury and damage to the motorcycle.

What about David's son, you ask, and other examples of severity in the Bible? I believe several things are true, and you can weigh each for yourself.

The Jews of the Old Testament attributed everything to God. We see this belief in Job's friends, who were so quick to accuse Job of being a terrible sinner to be punished so severely *by God*. However, when reading the whole story, we learn that it was Satan who brought loss, destruction, and physical harm to Job.

Some Scriptures that people use to cast God as the one who doles out punishment are written from the perspective of one in the middle of trouble or heartache, crying out to God their feelings. (In other words, their accusations against God are not factual, but rather what they think or feel because of their dire circumstances.) When we read the Bible, we need to discern between what God says about Himself and what the writers were feeling at the time.

Some Scriptures are also written prophetically about Jesus. Psalm 22 is a prime example; in it, David cries out, asking God why He has abandoned him. God had not really abandoned David, as he comes to realize and acknowledge in the latter part of this psalm. Christ spoke these same words from the cross, making it one of the many Old Testament prophecies Jesus fulfilled. There are many more examples in this psalm alone.

The Jewish people were so accustomed to attributing the

painful circumstances of life to God's judgment that Jesus had to directly confront this belief in His disciples. See John 9:1–3 (NIV):

> As he went along, he saw a man blind from birth. His disciples asked him, "Rabbi, who sinned, this man or his parents, that he was born blind?"
>
> "Neither this man nor his parents sinned," said Jesus, "but this happened so that the works of God might be displayed in him."

There are times when God judges wickedness and acts to stop it. I'm not saying any differently. But I believe these instances are exceptionally rare, as evidenced by all the evil that prevails in this world, of which Jesus said Satan is the ruler.

Yet for those of us who know and love God and still fail, for those of us who did not know Him in the past and failed; for our friends and family members who do not walk with the Lord and for whom we cry out to God for salvation of their eternal souls, I believe these verses from the book of Joel reveal God's heart (2:12–13, emphasis mine):

> "Even now," declares the LORD, "return to me with all your heart, with fasting and weeping and mourning." Rend your heart and not your garments. Return to the LORD your God, for he is *gracious* and *compassionate, slow to anger* and *abounding in love*, and *he relents from sending calamity*.

Psalm 103:8–18 (NIV) also reveals God's heart:

> The LORD is compassionate and gracious,
> slow to anger, abounding in love.
> He will not always accuse,
> nor will he harbor his anger forever;
> he does not treat us as our sins deserve

> or repay us according to our iniquities.
> For as high as the heavens are above the earth,
> so great is his love for those who fear him;
> as far as the east is from the west,
> so far has he removed our transgressions from us.
> As a father has compassion on his children,
> so the LORD has compassion on those who fear him;
> for he knows how we are formed,
> he remembers that we are dust.
> The life of mortals is like grass,
> they flourish like a flower of the field;
> the wind blows over it and it is gone,
> and its place remembers it no more.
> But from everlasting to everlasting
> the LORD's love is with those who fear him,
> and his righteousness with their children's children —
> with those who keep his covenant
> and remember to obey his precepts.

And the New Testament is filled to the brim with the evidence of God's mercy being poured out, as we have already seen.

God's deepest desire is *never* to punish us for our sins and failures, no matter how atrocious they are. His deepest desire is for us to genuinely repent, grieve our sin, *return* (or turn for the first time) to Him, and allow Him to pour out His grace, compassion, patience, and love upon us in measures that we simply cannot fathom.

There is a metaphor I liked to share with my ladies in jail who often felt that being incarcerated, losing parental rights, being fined, and the like were God's punishment and evidence of His lack of love, mercy, and forgiveness. They felt they deserved His anger and mistook consequences for their choices as His hand of vengeance against them.

Most of those ladies were moms, so I would set this story up as a mother relating to her little child:

Let's say you have a four-year-old child. You have been diligent in teaching them that they are not to touch the stove in your kitchen, explaining that it gets very hot and could hurt them badly. As most children do, the child decides to test you on this. They have sneaked in a few quick touches here and there, all with zero consequences. The times you have caught them doing so, you knelt down, forced them to look you in the eyes, and explained that while the stove was not hot *that* time, it does in fact get hot, in which case they would be burned, and it would hurt![6]

Then one day, it happens. Your little child approaches the stove just after you turned the burner off and firmly plants their tiny palm and fingers on the red-hot metal. Flesh is seared, and screams reverberate through your home and through your heart.

But you told them not to! You explained over and over again. Perhaps you made them sit in a corner or even smacked their hand for their disobedience, but in the end, they rebelled against you and your "rules."

At this point, I would ask the ladies what they would do—that is, what would a good, loving mother do? Before they have the chance to respond, I rush ahead saying, "I know! You would severely spank that child for being disobedient. Right?" This was usually met with looks of confusion and horror, as they

---

6. This is what God does in His Word when He warns us against all manner of sins. He explains why we should or should not do something, and His heart is always to protect and bless us.

didn't know exactly how to respond to their usually more sensible Bible study leader.

We would all conclude that a good parent would never inflict more pain upon this rebellious child. Rather, we would run to them, pick them up, and rush them to medical treatment. All the while, tears may be streaming down the mother's face as she tries to comfort her child, easing their pain to the best of her ability and telling them repeatedly that "Mommy is here. It's going to be okay. Mommy loves you. Oh, little one, this is why Mommy told you not to touch the stove. I'm so sorry this happened! I would take the pain for you if I could!"

This is a picture of our good, good Father. If you and I, in all our brokenness and sin, would never stoop to cause our beloved child pain over and above the natural consequences of their disobedience, how could we believe that our good, perfect, holy, loving-without-limits God would do such a thing?

Just like the mother in our story, God warns and pleads with us to be obedient. And when we, like the little child in the story, choose to go our own way, He swoops us up in His strong, loving embrace and comforts us, stays with us as we endure the consequences, and miraculously, if we allow Him to, works it out for our good.

We learn of the love behind His commands, to have compassion for others who fail, and, empowered by His Holy Spirit within us, to be more obedient in the future. Not out of fear of His anger or harsh punishment but out of such love for Him that we desire to follow His commands. We learn to trust in His goodness that only wants what is best for us so that we choose His way over ours, even when we don't understand why.

Chapter 16
No Condemnation

After personal failure, we tend to condemn ourselves and believe that God condemns us as well. Condemnation from others, a lack of compassion from those who profess to love God, and judgment and rejection from Christ's Body (the church) can convince us that God takes some kind of perverted joy in causing us pain, in rubbing our noses in our mistakes, in turning His back on us and leaving us to fend for ourselves.

I would like to share a portion of one more book with you. In fact, I recommend the whole book, although it is written from a strong Calvinistic viewpoint that I do not share.[7] Some of

---

7. If you would like to learn more, look up Calvinism versus Arminianism. As I stated earlier in this book, I wholeheartedly believe that God Almighty is sovereign! For Arminians, that means He is the absolute authority. He is King of kings, Lord of lords, the one and only true, living, omniscient, omnipotent, omnipresent God. Arminians also believe that God gave humans free will, that we live in a broken world, and that Satan is alive and has great power in this world for the time being. Thus, as we have previously discussed, God does not will or cause everything that happens in this world. Tragedy, illness, sin, natural disasters, and so on do not come from His hand

the author's beliefs about the sovereignty of God are, I believe, false. Because of this, I was a bit hesitant to read it myself. Not because I disagree or only read what echoes my beliefs. I honestly like to be challenged, and there have been times when I have been challenged enough to change not my core beliefs, but my understanding or interpretation of certain Scriptures.

That said, if you, dear reader, believe that God is disappointed in you . . . that He is ashamed of you. . . That His love and longing for you ever wavers according to your behavior. That your sin angers Him. That He pulls away from you when you grieve Him. If you ever feel like you have to both earn and maintain God's love, mercy, grace, forgiveness. If you feel abandoned by God in a pit of despair that you jumped into all on your own. If you feel God might freely forgive those who don't know Him, or those who know less than you, or those who have had it worse than you, or anyone else, but that He is less forgiving when it comes to you because you know better, you have made the same mistake too many times, you chose to go back where you knew you did not belong, you hurt too many people, you caused too much damage that can never be undone. . . Because God can't forgive *you* of that, whatever *that* might be. Or perhaps you believe He has forgiven but will also punish you and keep His distance.

If this is you, then I cannot recommend this book highly enough: *Gentle and Lowly: The Heart of Christ for Sinners and Sufferers* by Dane Ortlund.

I wish I had read this book long ago. I also wish I could fully and confidently embrace the fundamental truths in this book

---

but are consequences of our choices/sins, others' choices/sins, living in a broken world, and the very real spiritual realm of darkness that is allowed influence and power until Christ's return.

(notwithstanding the Calvinism). But sixty-three years of ingrained opinions take time to dismantle. Thus, I have marked up this book, as I always do, and will return to it over and over again to remind myself of the freeing truths about God's heart for me—*even* me—that Dane reveals through abundant scriptural references about God's heart of mercy, grace, compassion, and love when we are at our worst.

Because I can only quote so much, I beg you to buy this book and read it! Here are just a few of the most powerful excerpts:

> Perhaps you have difficulty receiving the rich mercy of God in Christ not because of what others have done to you but because of what you've done to torpedo your life, maybe through one big stupid decision or maybe through ten thousand little ones. You have squandered his mercy, and you know it.
>
> To you I say, do you know what Jesus does with those who squander his mercy? He pours out more mercy. God is rich in mercy. That's the whole point. . .
>
> It means the things about you that make you cringe most, make him hug hardest. . .
>
> It means our haunting shame is not a problem for him, but the very thing he loves most to work with.
>
> It means our sins do not cause his love to take a hit. Our sins cause his love to surge forward all the more.
>
> It means on that day when we stand before him, quietly, unhurriedly, we will weep with relief, shocked at how impoverished a view of his mercy-rich heart we had. . .[8]

---

8. Dane Ortlund, *Gently and Lowly: The Heart of Christ for Sinners and Sufferers*, pp. 178–80.

[W]hat does the gospel say. . . ? His heart for me could not sit still in heaven. Our sins darken our feelings of his gracious heart, but his heart cannot be diminished for his own people due to their sins any more than the sun's existence can be threatened due to the passing of a few wispy clouds or even an extended thunderstorm. The sun is shining. It cannot stop. Clouds, no clouds — sin, no sin — the tender heart of the Son of God is shining on me. This is an unflappable affection.

And the sweep of the New Testament teaching is that it is the sun of Christ's heart, not the clouds of my sins, that now defines me. When we are united to Christ, Christ's punishment at the cross becomes my punishment. In other words, the end-time judgment that awaits all humans has, for those in Christ, already taken place. We who are in Christ no longer look to the future for judgment, but to the past; at the cross, we see our punishment happening, all our sins being punished in Jesus. The loved and restored you therefore trumps, outstrips, swallows up, the unrestored you. Not the other way around.[9]

Dear reader, I implore once again, that if you struggle knowing and living from a place of loving acceptance from God, if you envision His face distorted in anger and rage, hand raised to strike, or His back turned toward you in cold rejection. . . If this is how you envision the Father's response to your failure, poor choices, pain and suffering, please do two things:

First and foremost, please look up Scriptures that speak of God's mercy and grace, compassion and forgiveness. Write them out. Speak them aloud. Work to memorize them and allow God to work mightily in your heart as you marinate in His Word. (You can find some in the back of this book.)

---

9. Ortlund, pp. 186–87.

Secondly, read Dane Ortlund's book. I am unable to reproduce here all the lengthy passages I wish to share. Just reading Dane's words and Scriptures brings freedom. (And by the way, he has a PhD in New Testament studies. So if you find yourself, and rightfully so, saying "Nancy Jo is okay, but she is lacking in the theology department," you may find the extra assurance you need in reading Dane's book.)

I have spent the great majority of my life living from the mindset of God's grace, mercy, and compassion being stingy rather than overflowing. Because of this erroneous understanding, this grotesque *mis*understanding of who God is and His heart toward me at all times, I have suffered. I have endured shame; I have been burdened by the enemy's condemnation; I have worked to try to be worthy of the favor of God; and as a result, I have responded to others' failures from a place of judgment and withdrawal.

We are all, every moment of every day, desperate for the amazing grace and fresh mercy of our heavenly Father. Let us, each one, revel in a new, more complete understanding that He delights in pouring out on us—not just what we need, but in overflowing abundance. We may be dry, but He does not portion out a drop or two of grace, or even an entire gallon of mercy. No! Not our good, good Father. Not our beloved Jesus. He scoops us up in His everlasting, loving arms and places us under the Niagara Falls of His unending grace, mercy, forgiveness, compassion, and love.

Oh, what a Savior! What amazing love! Let's get drenched, dear ones, and go about dripping all over others what has been so lavishly and freely poured out upon us.

We have hope because of the amazing goodness of our God. And because of His heart for us that never wavers, never wanes, never looks away. He never raises His eyebrows or shakes His head in disbelief or disgust. No, He always runs to us. Ready to comfort and restore the moment we repent and fall into His arms.

Consequences may be brutal. But He will walk with us through them every step of the way, working to transform us into the image of Jesus and to bless us beyond our wildest imaginations! Oh, how He loves us!

V.
Transformed

Chapter 17
Evidence of His Presence

Let's carry on in our journey toward our destination: Hope. As we travel, we grow in our ability to recognize God's hand and look for His presence in our lives. Like seeds, the evidence of His presence produces hope. It is a beautiful thing to see all God does for us.

1. He comforts us.

As God walks with us, He comforts us. Sometimes we are comforted as we read His Word. Sometimes we feel a literal physical presence, warmth, or pressure. Sometimes He speaks to our heart through the Holy Spirit. Often this comfort comes through others, but it is always ultimately from Him.

I am not a wonderful gardener. But our daughter, Rebekah, was! I always said she inherited her Grandmother Gibson's green thumb. I do, however, love flowers. Rebekah and I would have so much fun choosing flowers, planting them, enjoying their beauty, and even cutting and sharing them with others.

One year, we picked out a variety of Gerbera daisies. The colors were brilliant, and they made such lovely gifts to take to others. Even after cutting them, the blooms remained fresh for quite a while.

Gerbera daisies are not perennials. We knew that, but they were worth buying because we enjoyed them so much. And yet, we never had to buy them again! I am not sure if it was the nice bed of mulch we had, or if they enjoyed the heat radiating off our brick house, or if it was God's gift to us, but those daisies bloomed year after year after year. It was amazing, and we never failed to get excited and be amazed at their reappearance.

They continued to bloom each late spring or early summer . . . until the year after Rebekah was murdered in January 2009. Spring came and went, and there were no Gerbera daisies. Early summer arrived, and still nothing. It is hard to convey, or even understand myself, the loss and grief I felt knowing there would be no more daisies that Rebekah and I had planted and enjoyed so much together. Rational or not, the sorrow was acute.

One Sunday in the early summer, I was grieving Rebekah so very deeply. Barely able to speak through my sobs, I called my sister Reneé, and she came over to be with me instead of going to church. I was in my pajamas, I remember, my eyes and face red and swollen after hours of crying.

Reneé was just getting ready to leave when a strange car pulled into our driveway. I retreated down the hall and asked her to get the door because I was such a mess.

Moments later, Reneé called me to come and see who was here: Rebekah's dearly loved art teacher, Carolyn Coiner. She said that I had been on her mind, and she just wanted to stop by and let me know she was praying for me. In her arms was a beautiful potted Gerbera daisy! I had never in my life been given a Gerbera daisy before! Through tears, I shared the significance of this most amazing gift.

I continue to be struck by the tender, precious, intricate care of our heavenly Father! Out of all the flowers she could have chosen—out of all the days she could have come—God prompted Carolyn to choose the flower He knew would minister to my soul and to come on a day when I was in desperate need of the reminder that He loved me and was with me.

That little Gerbera daisy was planted and enjoyed all summer, and each summer you will find Gerbera daisies in front of my house. None have ever bloomed again the following year. I guess that was a special treat just for Rebekah and me.

Genesis 16:13 (AMP): "Then she called the name of the Lord who spoke to her, "You are God Who Sees'; for she said, 'Have I not even here [in the wilderness] remained alive after seeing Him [who sees me with understanding and compassion]?"

Years after this, in 2013, I was feeling kind of down on my birthday. It is extremely difficult to face birthdays when your child has no more. Once again, rationalization says that's kind of silly. But my mama-heart struggled, nonetheless, with feelings of heightened grief.

I was outside on the morning of my birthday, August 30, watering my flowers. And while there were most certainly Gerbera daisies, it was while I was watering huge pots of impatiens that I was speaking to the Lord. I cannot remember my exact words, but it was about my continued grief. I asked for a special gift that I would recognize as from Him. I was not only missing my child but also my beloved daddy on this birthday, and I just needed the comfort of a Father's love.

That afternoon, I received an email. More than ten years have passed, and I still get emotional just thinking about it. It was from Luanne Pierce, a lady I had never met in person but who had interviewed me over the phone for a magazine article at least weeks—perhaps months—before.

I still have the email. The subject heading reads "Happy Birthday!" At the top is a vibrant photograph of impatiens! Light and dark purples, oranges, and fuchsia pinks, with specks of brilliant green. The scripture beneath the photograph is Zephaniah 3:17 (ESV): "The Lord your God is in your midst, a mighty one who will save; He will rejoice over you with gladness; He will quiet you by His love; He will exult over you with loud singing."

This dear vessel of the Most High wrote:

> Happy Birthday, Nancy Jo!
>
> This morning, I was watering my impatiens and talking to the Father when He reminded me that today is your birthday. Have a spectacularly wonderful day!
>
> It's not that big a deal to get birthday greetings from me, but I just had to tell you that God Himself is thinking of you today, Nancy Jo. What an honor!

It has been almost twelve years since I received that birthday gift from God, and I have had to repeatedly wipe the tears from my eyes as I have written about it today. Luanne's closing was "May today be your best birthday yet!" Her sweet wish has also been granted. I will never forget and pray I will never cease to treasure the intimate gift of God's love on that very special day!

"Oh, how He loves us," as the song says.

The infinite, unchanging, powerful, glorious love of God is for each of us! May the truth of His love, His unwavering attention to every detail of our lives, and the whispers of our hearts cause us to never, ever doubt His goodness and faithfulness. He is always working and serves to give us hope as we trust in Him alone!

Psalm 33:20–22:

> Our hope is in the Lord.
> He is our help and shield.
> In him our hearts rejoice,
> For we trust in his holy name.
> Let your unfailing love surround us, LORD,
> For our hope is in You alone.

Even when we are comforted by others, God is the source of that comfort. He placed us on that person's heart and led them to show up or say/do what was such a blessing and help to us in our time of need.

2 Corinthians 1:3: "All praise to God, the Father of our Lord Jesus Christ. God is our merciful Father and the source of all comfort."

I remember when David's cousin came to visit one day. We sat in my living room, and I cried. She had also lost a child, her oldest son, just a few years before. I am positive the Lord gave her these words, for they impacted me greatly, and I have shared them many times with others, and they always bring comfort: "Rebekah is worthy of your grief."

Six simple words that were so freeing in the truth they contained.

2. God corrects us.

He does so with such kindness and love. He does so without accusation or condemnation, which are from the enemy. But He loves us too much not to correct us when we are wrong. And His correction, if we receive it, always brings freedom and joy.

I remember driving down the road many years ago, fussing up a storm to the Lord about David. I have no idea what the issue at the time was, but I was complaining to God and, most likely, I'm sorry to say, telling Him to please *do something* about him!

After my tirade, I remember hedging, "And I really do love David, Lord!" I heard the Holy Spirit so clearly: *"Oh. Really?"* (I do believe from moments such as this that God has a most wonderful sense of humor!) He continued, *"I thought love was patient and kind. I didn't think love kept a record of wrongs..."*

Yes, Lord. You're right. I'm sorry.

And, as with comfort, God will correct us through other people. He can even use people we do not particularly care for and people who don't even know Him to correct us. May I just say, it's one thing to be corrected in private by our kind, merciful, heavenly Father. It is a whole different ball game to be corrected by a person, *especially* if that person is not one of your favorite people.

And sometimes God uses your spouse. Why is it, I wonder, that my hackles rise dangerously when David corrects me, being that I generally receive correction well? It's something

I'm working on and have actually made good improvement in, thanks to the Lord and oftentimes a gentle approach on my husband's part.

3. God transforms us.

Down in that deep, dark pit of mud and mire, God is able to do miraculous work in our hearts, minds, and souls, *if* we will allow Him to. I guess this is a natural result of correction in general. Whereas a human being can correct/teach us and then we do with it what we will, when God corrects us, He also empowers us through the Holy Spirit to become more like Jesus—again, only *if* we cooperate with the work He wants to do in us.

David and I have shared openly and honestly, with great regret and sorrow, that who we were before the pit of grief and who we are now are miles apart. Miles for the better—for becoming more like Jesus: kinder, gentler, more grace-filled, more forgiving, and more merciful.

The truth is, we are not transformed into the image of Christ when things are rosy and easy. Sure, we might make some progress then. But it is in the pit when we cling to God and realize He is clinging to us. God is all the hope we really have when our whole world falls down around us, leaving us shattered and crumpled, wounded so gravely that it feels hard to put one foot in front of the other. It is there—in the furnace, in the raging ocean, in the pain and suffering, the grief and agony, the instability and uncertainty—that we come to the place where we say, perhaps something as simple as, "God, I can't. . ."

What comes next is unique to every pit: "God, I can't forgive, go back and fix it, see how I will ever make it, take this pain anymore, believe I'll ever change, believe he or she will ever change, believe You really love me/forgive me/can redeem this . . . God, I can't, but I believe *You* can. I believe You want to! I *believe*. . . Help me cooperate so You can."

Psalm 14:6 says, "The wicked frustrate the plans of the oppressed, but the LORD will protect his people."

This verse captivated me after Rebekah's death. I'm sharing it here, but you can see that it would fit in with correction as well. As a matter of fact, it just hit me: *If* we receive God's correction and agree to cooperate with Him, the end result is always transformation. Wow, I had never made that connection before!

I read Psalm 14:6 when I was in a season of fear over the upcoming trial and obsessing about justice for Rebekah. Upon my first read, I wrote in my Bible: "The wicked do have power, but God's is greater and His covering is over me."

I heard the Holy Spirit say, *"Read it again."* I did and came away with something deeper, which I also jotted down: "The wicked can frustrate my plans, but they cannot touch God's plans for me." So true. But once again, that still, small voice spoke: *"Read it again, Nancy Jo."*

With the third reading, I believe my eyes opened to what God wanted me to take away from that little but multilayered verse: I wrote, "I alone can frustrate God's plans for me when I refuse to be obedient to Him." Indeed, we can frustrate God's plans for us when we refuse to be obedient to Him.

That was a powerful revelation to me! Neither the defense attorney, judge, jury, murderer—not even Satan himself through Rebekah's death or anything else—was powerful enough to block God's plans for me. But I was.

It still packs a punch when I stop and think about it. God's plan for all those who call Him Father, who follow Jesus as Savior and Lord, is to make us more like Jesus. To make us holy and righteous and victorious over sin. For us to have an abundant life of joy, peace, and hope. For us to live in freedom, not enslaved to this world or our flesh. *This* is God's "very good" plan for you and for me.

And just as nothing in all creation, neither angels nor demons, life nor death, worries nor fears can ever separate us from God's love in Christ Jesus, so nothing—neither disaster or loss or sickness or grief or pain or betrayal—can annul God's plans for us. *Except* when we choose willful disobedience. While even rebellion cannot permanently derail God's plans of blessings and life for us, we can certainly frustrate those good plans as we reap the consequences of willful sin in our lives.

In that dark, dank, horrible pit, however, we have a golden opportunity to submit to God, cling to His promises, and allow Him to do a work in us that is utterly miraculous. It is a painful process, but it has a glorious resolution! While David and I are certainly nowhere near the godly reflections of Jesus that we long to be, we are so much more like Him than we were. Our oldest son, Davy, has said, "Daddy, Mama, you are so different!" And when your adult son sees the transformation, it is real!

Allow God to transform your pit from a place of utter helplessness, void of hope, to a place where you allow Him to work in you in mighty ways. Allow Him to fill you with the hope that when He finally lifts you out of that pit, you are going to more genuinely reflect His character to those around you!

It is usually only when looking back that we can see how God has gone before us. And even when we can look back on other times when God went before us, it is in the midst of on-going trial, tragedy, fear, unrest, and instability that it feels like we are alone.

Psalm 40:1: "I waited patiently for the LORD to help me, and he turned to me and heard my cry."

Did you catch that? "He turned to me." God is with us in the pit of despair! We are not alone.

I believe there are things we can do to maintain hope while we are enduring difficulties. Let's explore these together.

Chapter 18
Humility

How can humility on our part impact our hope? Let's look at it from the reverse side first: How does pride negatively impact our hope?

Remember when I told God to tell Rebekah what to pray for in heaven? Remember me trying to control David? These scenes are evidence of the pride that relentlessly seeks to invade my mind and soul.

There is no peace when I think I am in control. None! Why? Because there are relentless reminders that I am actually not in control! Not of others, not of my health, not of situations, not of the weather, not of other drivers on the road. . . Let's face it—I have a hard enough time controlling *myself*: I eat too much, stay up too late reading books, forget anything that is not written down and sometimes things that *are* written down . . . and yet I somehow think I am a good candidate to be in control of important things? If it weren't so sad, the absurdity of it would be hysterical. But I can't help but imagine what a slap in the face this attitude is to my heavenly Father.

There is no peace when I try to help God or try to confine Him to my timetable or my boxes. Often, my most ingenious helps, my most brilliant and well-thought-out boxes, are dismal failures. When my "help" isn't accepted, I get insulted and angry. When my boxes are not filled, I get depressed and hopeless.

In the seasons when we most need buoyant hope (like the Sandra Bullock movie *Hope Floats*), it follows that we are weighed down. We are already burdened with grief, loss, uncertainty, pain, and pressure. Pride does nothing to alleviate this weight but, instead, multiplies it exponentially.

Consider this quote from C. S. Lewis:

> The essential vice, the ultimate evil is pride. Unchastity, greed, drunkenness and all that are mere flea bites in comparison. It was through pride that the devil became the devil. Pride leads to every other vice: It is the complete anti-God state of mind.

Several years after Rebekah's murder, David and I were struggling in our marriage. We had always struggled to a certain extent. With grief, which we processed differently, as well as the trauma and stress that emotionally drained us, there wasn't much left over to process disagreements. It was during this dark, almost hopeless time that we went to see an excellent counselor (our third). In our first session, after we each shared, the counselor gave David some pretty tough-to-swallow observations and strict directions. I left feeling really good. *This* counselor was going to be able to help us. He told it like it was and, while kind, didn't mince words.

We returned a week later. I honestly do not remember anything about the conversation that day except the following, which is forever etched on my soul. At one point, the counselor looked at me and, just as he had to David, spoke not unkindly but very directly: "You are full of self-righteousness and pride."

Ouch! Ouch! *Ouch!* Not only would I have never relished hearing those words, they struck an even harsher blow because I thought I had come so far in ridding pride and self-righteousness from my heart since Rebekah's death and all the Lord had taught me. Plus, it was just plain . . . humiliating.

My first impulse was to think that this counselor wasn't so great after all. Ha! No, in all seriousness, his words, while cutting me to the quick, were able to peel back my incorrect assumptions about how far I had come in eliminating pride and self-righteousness from my life. It had to be exposed for there to be more change, more healing. For me to become more like my humble Savior and, thus, a better wife, mother, friend, and a more hope-filled person.

Philippians 2:3: "Don't be selfish; don't try to impress others. Be humble, thinking of others as better than yourselves."

Such simple sentences. Such simple *commands*. There is not a word or a phrase that you and I cannot understand in this little verse. And yet, to be honest, I have to keep these words before me all the time! I have to consciously choose to examine myself when with someone or in a situation that is causing me irritation/aggravation/frustration. To expose, as that excellent counselor did, my potentially hidden motives or thoughts that center around pride.

There are times after prayer and asking the Lord to examine my heart, after being quiet in His presence, that I can look at a situation and know I am not at fault in any way. These are exceptionally rare cases, but they have happened. Several times . . . well, at least twice that I can think of! But in all sincerity, even when the problem does not lie in me, this verse, along with Colossians 3:12–15, works well to give me the desire to either work within the situation or walk away with a humble heart. And with no ill will, birthed and nurtured in an ugly heart of pride and self-righteousness.

Think about it. Arguments, one-upmanship, having to be right and making sure others *know* we are right, worrying about what others think of us, wanting to be sure we have more—attention, stuff, power, love, recognition—the inability to make (or admit to making) mistakes. . . Does any of this lead to hope? On the contrary, they suck hope right out of us.

Why? Because they are rooted in lies. And they are masks that are awfully heavy to wear. They get heavier and heavier the more years we struggle to hide or rationalize more and more failures on our part. They become stiff and rigid barriers that prevent others from knowing the real us: flaws and all. And the ironic thing about it is that rather than drawing others to us, our inauthenticity repels them. (More on this in a bit.)

I found the following prayer by Cardinal Rafael Merry del Val years ago. I have modified it to make it my own over the years. My additions are in brackets. And there are a lot of variations on this prayer if you look it up online.

A Private Litany of Humility

From the desire of being praised, deliver me, Jesus.
From the desire of being honored, deliver me, Jesus.
From the desire of being preferred, deliver me, Jesus.
From the desire of being consulted, deliver me, Jesus.
From the desire of being approved, deliver me, Jesus.
From the desire for comfort and ease, deliver me, Jesus.
[From the desire to be "right," deliver me, Jesus.
From the desire to control, deliver me, Jesus.
From the propensity to climb onto a seat of judgment, deliver me, Jesus.]

From the fear of being humiliated, deliver me, Jesus.
From the fear of being criticized, deliver me, Jesus.
From the fear of being passed over, deliver me, Jesus.
From the fear of being forgotten, deliver me, Jesus.
From the fear of being lonely, deliver me, Jesus.
From the fear of being hurt, deliver me, Jesus.
From the fear of pain and suffering, deliver me, Jesus.
[From the fear of being taken advantage of, deliver me, Jesus.
From the fear of being rejected, deliver me, Jesus.
From the fear of admitting failures and mistakes and the slowness of confessing to others and seeking forgiveness from You, deliver me, Jesus.]

That others may be loved more than I, Jesus, grant me the grace to desire it.
That others may be chosen and I set aside, Jesus, grant me the grace to desire it.
That others may be praised, and I unnoticed, Jesus, grant me the grace to desire it.

O Jesus, meek and humble of heart, make my heart like Yours.
O Jesus, meek and humble of heart, strengthen me with Your Spirit.
O Jesus, meek and humble of heart, teach me Your ways.
O Jesus, meek and humble of heart, help me put my self-importance aside to learn the kind of cooperation with others that makes possible the presence of Your Abba's household.
Amen.[10]

You may wonder, what good does a litany like this do? Good question. I am not one who gravitates to pre-written prayers. But I have to say that this one is powerful, and God has truly used it to do the following:

---

10. Adapted from a prayer by Rafael, Cardinal Merry Del Val, from the prayer book *For Jesuits*, 1963, Loyola University Press, https://orientations.jesuits.ca/humility.html.

- make me aware of pride and habitual mindsets that would otherwise go unnoticed,
- bring conviction and repentance when I see myself in the words,
- help me recognize prideful attitudes and thoughts before I embrace them,
- and (I am *so* happy to say) see improvement in my life.

I used to pray this litany every day, using it to examine myself over the previous twenty-four hours. I would confess all the ways I did not allow Jesus to deliver me. And the desire for Jesus, meek and humble of heart, to make my heart like His became a genuine heart cry and a focus for me throughout each day.

It's embarrassing to share, but I remember when our youngest granddaughter, Audrey Joy, was tiny. (She's a big girl of three now!) Of all our granddaughters (we have six!), Audrey Joy decided she preferred Granddaddy (David) over Mom-Mom (me). Can I just be honest and say I didn't much like that? All the girls were Mom-Mom girls! Of course, I didn't say anything or act in any way that others would see my feelings. But those feelings were there. As I said, I am genuinely embarrassed, but it irked me.

Thankfully, I recognized my pride quickly, and although I had "graduated" from praying through the humility litany every day, I got it back out and moved it to my daily stack. When I got it out the next time and read, "That others may be loved more than I, Jesus, grant me the grace to desire it," boy, did the Lord convict me! I began to do all I could to not only change my feelings but also nurture and encourage Audrey Joy's love for her granddaddy. And guess what! I began to receive much joy out witnessing that special bond. I still do. In times like that, I pull the litany back out, and it becomes part of my daily Scripture work again. For me, pride is an insidious evil that I have to be on guard against at all times. But I can't begin to tell you the gratitude and joy I experience when I realize, "Hey, I haven't done that for quite a while. I have not had/acted on that desire. I have not submitted to that fear. Jesus! You are strengthening me with the Holy Spirit; You are teaching me; You are making my heart like Yours. Thank You, thank You!"

Pride makes us callous and often causes others to view us as inaccessible. Oh, the freedom in not trying to "be all that," in not trying to climb on a pedestal, and in not trying to balance atop one either. The freedom! The authenticity! The rest! The joy and laughter that flow from genuine humility and a desire to see others succeed, without worrying about appearances or trying to maintain an "I'm okay" veneer of control.

I had the most wonderful partner when I did jail ministry with women who were incarcerated for anything from writing bad checks to DUIs to murder. My partner, Nancy, and I had so much fun together and were so blessed to be able to love on the ladies in our class. We repeatedly said that we learned as much from them as they could ever learn from us.

One year, Nancy and I came up with a game to play in our last class before Christmas. It would take time away from the lesson, but jail is an unhappy place, and we wanted to let the ladies have some laughter along with their learning.

The game was simple: Nancy had written down Christmas song titles on little slips of paper. We explained that one person from each team would come up to receive one of these slips. She had, say, two minutes to help her team guess the song without saying any words in the title. If they answered correctly, she could keep going, helping her team guess as many song titles as possible within the time limit.

We needed to divide the ladies into two groups. It was an odd number, so it was determined that I would play on one of the teams. There were two ladies we were afraid would not participate. One in particular was exceptionally shy, rarely saying much of anything or participating in any way. We did not want to make this stressful for either, so we let them know that they did not have to be the one giving clues if they didn't want to, but we hoped that everyone would help their team in guessing the songs.

My team was up first, and I was the first person to give the clues. This was when God showed up in the most hilarious of ways!

I drew the first song title: "Grandma Got Run Over by a Reindeer." Even though I helped define the rules, I completely forgot that I could speak. Nancy said, "Go!" and I proceeded to act like a grandma, then like a reindeer running around the room, making antlers with my hands. Then, again as the grandma, I looked up in shock and fell on the floor.

This went on and on and on, with zero correct guesses. I wish I had a video recording! To this day, I wonder what the guards who watched the cameras were thinking; they could have blackmailed me with the security footage that day, if they'd wanted to.

When time was up, I was laughing, out of breath, and had not won a single point for my team. The ladies were laughing with me, and when Nancy told them the title, they said they thought all the songs would be "Christian."

I still laugh when I think of that day, but I also tear up when I remember what happened afterward: Every single one of those ladies, including the sweet, shy gal we just knew would not participate, joined in both guessing and giving clues. Why wouldn't they? There was no way they could do any worse than their teacher! Surely they could get points using words. And even if they didn't, so what!

While I did not intentionally make a fool of myself, I was completely unconcerned about what anyone thought of me. By humbling myself in this way, I'm in awe of the results. I doubt those ladies will ever forget my shenanigans! I know Nancy remembers, and I believe she even tells her current ministry groups the story as a way of breaking the ice and reminding them that they *can* use words during the game.

There was so much laughter that day! And every time I am reminded of God's intervention—that we had an odd number of ladies, that I was the extra rather than Nancy, that I went first, that I picked that ridiculous song title, and that I forgot I could talk—I am touched by the sentiment as well as the humor. Think about how much God wanted every single one of those ladies to enjoy her fun escape from the reality of being in jail. Oh, how He loves that shy gal, that He would orchestrate everything to perfection to help her get over her fear of participating.

I can't help but think of Baalam's donkey. Like Baalam, I was completely oblivious to what God was up to, but He worked through my mistakes, my forgetfulness, and my inadequacies as much as my willingness to "let my hair down" and just be another gal having fun (perhaps making if not a reindeer, then a "donkey" of herself).

Rather than being embarrassed that I didn't score any points, and looked ridiculous rolling around on the floor to boot, I joined in the hysterics. I've laughed out loud just typing out this story!

Humility lets us laugh at ourselves. My father taught me this too. And my husband, David, has a brilliant, quick sense of humor. I've said he could be a stand-up comedian and never run out of material because I provide him so much!

I had major abdominal surgery in September 2023. I can be very self-conscious, and I am extremely private and modest. As such, in the hospital, I had some uncomfortable situations to navigate. My self-consciousness slipped away as I set modesty aside to be grateful for the kind, gentle care of nurses. I made sure to express my gratitude frequently and show interest in their lives.

One nurse and I laughed together over my "out-on-the-town" (or walking down the hall rather) ensemble. She said that when her mom had surgery, she refused to use the walker. I said, "Oh, but that's the best accessory—the finishing touch on the lovely hospital gown and paper panties!"

Life is so much better when we are humble rather than stuffed up and puffed up and stiff with pride. Better and more fun! Believe me, I know. I've tried it both ways.

Friend, this humility is honestly difficult for me. I am very self-conscious most of the time. It can be crippling, robbing me of enjoying whatever situation I might be in. I can get so focused on what others might think of me that I miss opportunities for God to work through my imperfections.

I want to be humble! I want to "think of others as better than myself." I want to not necessarily think less of myself (although sometimes that is required) but, as the saying goes, "to think of myself less."

From the fear of being humiliated, deliver me, Jesus! When we are willing to humble ourselves, God can do incredible things through us and in spite of us.

Humility reminds me that I am to focus on pleasing no one but God. Humility reminds me that I am to focus on what God wants to do in me, giving Him the freedom to correct and redirect me, and (probably the hardest, at least for me) to accept correction from others.

(Actually, I've gotten so much better at receiving correction . . . well, except maybe from my husband. But I'm even making progress there! Just ask him!)

Humility enables us to lay down our plans, our preferences, the way we think things should be "fixed," our boxes, and even our very selves and say, "Father God, Your will be done, in Your timing and in Your way."

Chapter 19
Openness

I had the honor of speaking at Stonecroft Ministries Women's Connection for several years after Rebekah's death. My mama was kind enough to accompany me on many of these trips so that I would not be on the road alone, especially when traveling out of state.

Mama is a shopper. I. Am. *Not.* At eighty-eight, she can still shop me under the table — or into a puddle on the floor, an image which probably captures it best. On one of our trips, she was determined to find a "little black dress" for me to speak in. And she did. The only problem, which I pointed out, was that it accentuated my belly pooch.

In my younger years (read pre-menopause), I was tiny. I could out-eat my six-foot, muscular husband and never gain a pound. Well, that all changed when I completed menopause at the ripe old age of thirty-seven. I went from having a stick figure to what I call a sturdy branch figure. I've never had curves, and I was (still am, to be honest) very self-conscious of my less-than-flat stomach.

But I *loved* the dress. Mama had the answer. SPANX shapewear! There were two different styles: one that came up above the bra and one that came just below the bra. Since I've never been well endowed, I didn't want to flatten the little bust I do have, so we got the below-bra style.

I gratefully took my dress and SPANX home and looked forward to my next speaking engagement, which was for a women's meeting in a different state. A few days before, I wanted to pick out the pair of shoes that would look best with the dress.

I got the little black dress out of the closet, along with the SPANX, and tried them on. Getting into the SPANX was somewhat of a challenge, but I managed it pretty well. As I looked at my reflection in the full-length mirror, I was amazed. I had curves! My stomach was flat, and my waist dipped in while my hips flared out in the way I had always wished. It was impressive, let me tell you! I was going to have to get more of those SPANX.

Now I just needed the right shoes. I turned sideways to head toward my closet, and out of the corner of my eye, I caught a glimpse of the back of the dress. It was sticking out in the middle of my back in a manner that was quite odd and noticeable. I thought, "What is wrong with this dress?" and "Why in the world did we not see this in the store?" It was that obvious.

I ran my hand up around my back and immediately discovered the problem. It was not the dress. The SPANX had squeezed all my fat up, and it was spilling over the top of the garment, making a bulge in the top back of the dress. Ugh! I was embarrassed even though I was all by myself!

Needless to say, the SPANX came off, never to be worn again. I did wear the dress, figuring a little belly pooch was better than a great big lump on my back!

As I mulled over this story, the Lord spoke some truths to my heart. I wonder if you can relate. . .

How often do we camouflage our "fat"? How often do we try to cover up our sorrows, failures, fears, and disappointments by wearing, if not SPANX, then a metaphorical costume or a mask? By pretending to have it all together. By refusing to be real and vulnerable.

I was disappointed that the SPANX didn't work for me; I don't want to diminish the fact that we should try to look our best. If it had worked, I'd probably be tempted to wear it all the time. But the Lord took the opportunity to talk to me about being "real."

For many years, I wore a metaphorical mask. I kept an air of having it all together when, in reality, I did not. Masks do that. When we keep them securely affixed, no one knows or even suspects the hurt, sorrow, frustration, temptations, failures, and fears we endure in private. When this happens, we see two results.

First, people cannot relate to us. They instinctively hide their problems because it seems like we don't have any and, therefore, could not understand or empathize with them. They either avoid us or don their own masks when they are around us. We come across in an intimidating manner, even if we don't mean to.

The second thing that can happen is that we think our masks, or shapewear, are securely in place, but it is quite clear to everyone else that the lumps and bumps in the back are not part of the outfit! They are our imperfections, and they are glaringly obvious. This is when others label us hypocrites. We lack authenticity. We lose the respect of the very people God would have us share His gift of hope with because they aren't interested in what we have to share.

Openness is of extreme importance if we want to have and to share hope. Because let's be honest: When I stood in front of that mirror admiring "my" hourglass figure, I knew it wasn't really me. So let's say there was no blatant lump on my back. Although I may have fooled everyone looking at me, as soon as I took off my dress and the undergarments, the reality would have been plain for me to see.

Let's dig a little deeper. There are those who will disagree with me here, but I'm asking you to hear me out: **Hope does not equate to a denial of reality.**

We do not have to live in denial of a terminal illness to have hope of healing! After all, if I refuse to admit I have cancer, how can I give God the glory for healing?[11]

This is a sore subject for me. I believe much damage has been done to Christians who have been told that if they only had "enough" faith, they would be healed. (My own dear daddy, who loved God with all his heart, trusted in God's love and goodness, and prayed for his healing and asked others to pray, was told that he did not have enough faith or he would have been healed of pain and able to walk.) Some are told that if they say the words, "I have cancer," then God will not heal

---

11. Is our hope in being healed of a disease, or is our hope in God who will be with us no matter what as we hope for healing in His name? Our certain hope is in knowing that nothing can separate us from His love, He can use all things for our good and His glory, and we *will* be healed—either here or in heaven.

them. Or that if healing is delayed, there must be some unconfessed sin in their lives.

Now please, *please* hear me: Scripture does say that embraced sin on our part, especially the sin of unforgiveness, hinders answered prayers (Mark 11:25). Scripture does tell us to have faith. But faith in what—in whom? We are now back to my original point. Our faith must be in God, and not in anything else, *including* what He might do for us.

Yes! Our faith must rest in God's character and promises. But I believe we sometimes misinterpret His promises. We covered this before, but let's go a bit further.

I shared the verses in Isaiah 43:1–3 that comforted me and include the following lines: "When you go through the fire of oppression, you will not be burned up. The flames will not consume you." Now I ask you: What about the early Christian martyrs who were burned alive? During the rule of the Romans, and even later in England, Christians were burned at the stake. Christians who loved Jesus and were martyrs for that very reason alone. What we do with this truth can help us when faced with our own fires.

Have there never been Christians who died in floods or drowned in bodies of water? ("When you go through deep waters, I will be with you. When you go through rivers of difficulty, you will not drown.") Did they lack faith or have unconfessed sin, or are we at risk of misinterpreting/misapplying this scriptural promise?

To help reckon with this, let's ask, what is God's main focus? Is it our flesh or our eternal soul? Does death equal the end of life or the beginning of perfect life in heaven and on what will be a brand-new earth?

After Rebekah's murder, I found that I could not say the words "Rebekah is dead." I could say, "Rebekah was murdered," or "We lost our daughter." Now I'm perfectly willing to admit that a counselor may have some insight into this, which I do not have, but this is what I do know:

The absolute truth, the *real* reality, is that my Rebekah is not dead. She is not lying in a grave. Yes, her body is there, but *she* is not! Rebekah is alive and well. She is with God. She is "perfectly happy and content"—not just while awaiting justice, but in every way possible.

I believe that we must—if we are going to be scripturally accurate, and if we are not going to give false assurances or place false blame—look at God's promises in light of eternity. God most certainly intervenes in this world: in our human bodies, in the weather, in natural and man-made disasters, in providing needs and even wants, and in too many ways to list here. But we must leave how and when He intervenes and all those other details in the loving, faithful, sovereign hands of our God, who is a good, good Father. Even when we do not understand His ways, like a little child who does not understand or interpret all of a good earthly father's decisions and actions.

We do not have to stuff our grief over the loss of a loved one to have hope in a God who promises to heal the brokenhearted and bind up their wounds. After all, if we have never received God's comfort, the Bible makes it pretty clear that we will have no comfort to offer others. We do not have to hide disappointment to have the hope of God working even in "this" for our good and His glory. A failure to share disappointments and heartaches with others is damaging to our relationships; it keeps them superficial.

Rather than hiding, denying, and stuffing, God gives us the

freedom to say, "Yes, I am in a pit—a nasty, dark, horrible pit! *But* I have a God who is with me and who promises to lift me out. And when He does, I am going to have such a testimony that tells of His goodness, faithfulness, and love!"

Fear of being open with others keeps us distant and always working and worrying about keeping our masks in place or our fat squished and smoothed down. It is exhausting work! Fear of being open with God keeps us from sharing our deepest, truest selves with Him. It keeps us from inviting Him to join us in the pit while we pretend to be walking outside of it. How can He meet our needs then?

Fear of being open with ourselves leads to pride, deception, and depression. Living outside of reality robs us of hope, for we have effectively isolated ourselves from God and others. God meets us where we are, not where we imagine ourselves to be.

It is when I am open with God and others and honest about my struggles that He will miraculously empower me. When I am not open with God—bringing my struggles, fears, and concerns to Him—I cut myself off from His help. And when I try to pretend, even to myself, that I am fine when I am not, I will eventually fall under the crushing weight of pretense. Why do we do this to ourselves? (Could it be pride?)

When I was on staff at my church, Church on the Hill in Fishersville, Virginia, I was blessed and honored to be asked to speak from time to time on Sunday mornings from the pulpit. As I would work on a sermon that exposed ugly truths about myself—heartbreaking mistakes and failures—in the hope and prayer that others would learn from my mistakes, I would suffer great trepidation, thinking, "I hope Pastor Brandon doesn't fire me! No one is going to like me or seek any counsel from such a broken mess!"

At first, it caught me by great surprise, but eventually, I realized a profound truth: When I shared my own failures, struggles, and mistakes and how God loved me and worked through them, people were drawn *to* me. They recognized me as a safe place, as another human being who loved God but didn't have it all together. And guess what. . . It gave them hope!

If God could set me free, He could set *them* free. If God could forgive me, He would forgive them. If God could transform me, He could transform them. If God could use me—a broken vessel—certainly He could use them. If God carried me, surely He would carry them.

Writing my first book was brutal. It was so hard to write out all my failures as a mother and relive the crushing onslaught of grief as I narrated the early days/months after Rebekah's death. I kept a tissue box by the computer as I would literally sob as I tried to type.

But it is only when I am open with others that they know how to pray for me. I had many brothers and sisters in Christ covering me in prayer as I agonized through the writing of Rebekah's and my story.

I'm not saying we share our deepest spiritual struggles with everyone we know. No, by all means, find a few trusted people who know you, love you, and love Jesus, and share with them.

Because here is the truth: When we hide sin and struggles, we give Satan power over us. We keep a part of ourselves in the dark, where he binds and restricts, rather than coming into the light where Christ can reign, rule, and bring freedom.

This is what I have found to be true when we (or someone we love) suffer a major failure or struggle: The temptation to hide it and keep it secret is huge! But evil people and even, I am sad to say, church people who do not allow the Holy Spirit to control their tongues, are going to find out eventually. They will be cruel and unkind. You can expect it.

When we hide our sins, struggles, and failures, what we actually do is rob ourselves of the wonderful people who will come alongside us, love us, encourage us, support us, pray for us to have victory, pick us up, and help us see that God is with us, even in the pit we may have made for ourselves.

Chapter 20
Presence

To have hope, we also must be diligent to remain in the present. Remember, God does go before us. But it is in the here and now that He is walking with us.

It is important to me that no one who ever reads this book or anything I write or who hears me speak thinks I have "graduated" from grief. Yes, the grief is no longer a constant crushing. Yes, my tears come less often. Yes, I am rarely down in the pit of grief for more than a day or two at a time. And for that, I thank the Lord! But there are still times when tears flow for most of my waking hours. There are still times when grief takes my breath away and saps my energy. There are still times when I am vulnerable to the enemy's attacks to steal my joy and hope.

On April 23, 2024, Rebekah would have turned thirty-six years old. Not only was I missing her tremendously, but I was once again vulnerable to the enemy's attacks and his desire to put me in the past, which I am utterly helpless to change. It was, to be honest, a horrible morning.

Then, a most precious friend and spiritual mother texted to

check in on me. This is what she wrote:

> I trust your sorrow is wrapped around missing Rebekah's presence and not residuals of painful guilt. We have those pain-ridden past experiences to help others stay out of the weeds of life. We mustn't allow the enemy any space to lay repented-for burdens on us. That can zap our joy for sure! We take our God-given authority over those dark works in Jesus' name. May joy flow abundantly for you on her birthday anniversary. May you revel in all God has taught by reason of your precious child. Things you would not know apart from your relationship with her! God always works all things in our lives together for His glory and our good. We can take those painful things into a glorious future of sharing and caring for others... I praise Him for His omnipotent grace!

This text was a lifeline to me that morning. Bettie's perception of exactly what I was facing, her spiritual insight and spot-on truths, her heart for me brought me right back to the present. And the truth that I am forgiven! I have confessed, and there is no reason to look back at my failures other than to learn from them or to help someone else.

"Repented-for burdens," as Bettie so aptly put it, are what we allow the enemy to pile on us: guilt over confessed sin that by God's grace we either still struggle with or are cooperating with Him to overcome and regret over things we have done or said that weren't sinful but seem to have led to catastrophe. We must stay in the present and refuse to let the enemy "zap our joy." We look for God's hand and thank Him for all He has done, even amid pain and heartache and loss. And as we remain in the present, we look forward to the opportunities we have every day to share and care for others.

That anointed text was a God-sent sermon to me that day. It corrected, challenged, and encouraged me. How grateful I was.

It drew my focus off my heavy, sorrow-filled, ugly, hopeless past and repositioned my thoughts in the present. And it was a present in which I could give thanks to God and be filled with the hope of knowing He was with me, right in that moment.

One day, some months after Rebekah's death, I was driving when I saw a young woman walking on the side of the road. She was tall, slender, with short dark hair; she looked like Rebekah. I was ambushed with grief. As I drove along, tears running down my face, I cried out, "Lord, I just can't get through this! I will never see Rebekah's face again. I will never hear her laugh. I will never hear her call and say, 'Mama!' I will never . . ."

The list was long, and each "never" was spoken with great anguish as I forced the words through an aching throat clogged with grief. I don't know how long this lasted, but I began to run out of "nevers." I heard the Lord call my name and ask in a gentle, tender voice, "Nancy Jo. Can you get through today?" I was a bit caught off guard, as I hadn't expected to hear anything in return. But in that slight pause, my soul settled a bit. I replied, out loud, "Yes, Lord, *with* You, I can get through today."

What a comfort! God reminded me in a moment of deep anguish that He was walking with me. He heard me, He did not ask the impossible of me, and He would help me. I understood that I was not to focus too far ahead but rather to make short-term progress, getting through one day at a time, holding tightly to Him and letting Him hold me.

You and I can imagine what the future might hold. But when we peer ahead with worry or dread of the unknown—or even what we do know lies ahead—we are incapable of imagining God in the picture. The future that we fear in our imaginings is one void of God.

It is best to stay in the present, and even then we can still plan for the future! We can and should sometimes look ahead to plan and make decisions to the best of our ability. But when it comes to anxiety-producing thoughts and mental scenarios of situations we have not yet experienced, it is best to refuse to go there and instead entrust our future to God.

How do we remain in the present?

We refuse to look at the past other than to learn from it or use it to teach/help someone else. Satan loves it when we fixate on our past regrets. Why? Because we can do nothing to change the past! And, on the opposite end of the spectrum, we have a tendency, like the Israelites wandering in the wilderness, to romanticize it. We long for what was while not remembering *all* that was—like roses without the sting of the thorns.

A longing for the past blinds us to the blessings God is pouring out upon us today. Sitting and stewing in regret brings despair rather than hope. If we are entombed in the past, we are unable to enjoy the blessings God has for us today.[12]

The best way I have found to guard my mind from looking back with shame, regret, or unhealthy longing is to practice Philippians 4:6–7:

> Don't worry about anything; instead, pray about everything. Tell

---

12. If this is something you struggle with, you may be interested to read Chapter 24 of my first book, in which I describe the on-going journey of finding freedom from regret.

God what you need, and thank him for all he has done. Then you will experience God's peace, which exceeds anything we can understand. His peace will guard your hearts and minds as you live in Christ Jesus.

Sometimes my "praying" looks like I am worrying God. Imagine a pitiful, perhaps even whiny voice: "O Lord, I just don't know what is going to happen! This is terrible, and that is awful! I can't do this, and they won't do that! And what in the world are we going to do about it?"

This is not the kind of prayer Paul is talking about here. Tell God what you need, or pray, "Lord, only You know what I need." Thank Him for what He has done and what He is doing (John 5:17). Our hope rests in the truth that God hears our prayers and knows what we need even before we do. Our hope rests in the evidence of all He has done for us in the past and the certainty that He will continue to work on our behalf.

We are not to sit and rehearse worst-case scenarios with God. We are not to dwell on what we don't know or can't do. It's okay to begin our conversations with God by laying out our worries, so long as we move past them (the quicker the better) to get to the "But God" part. What does that part look like? Paul tells us in verse 8:

> And now, dear brothers and sisters, one final thing. Fix your thoughts on what is true, and honorable, and right, and pure, and lovely, and admirable. Think about things that are excellent and worthy of praise.

Use these guidelines for what to think about. We start with what is *true*, but this must fit the other categories as well. I can focus on truths that do nothing to bring peace or hope. I call those "little-*t* truths": truths the enemy is fine pointing out to us, which, while accurate, steal our joy, hope, and peace. We must combat those little-*t* truths with what I call "Big-*T* Truths": truths that are based on God's character and promises, no matter what circumstantial, little-*t* truths abound at the moment.

> **little-*t* truth:** I no longer have a daughter to love here on earth! I miss her daily to the core of my being.
> **Big-*T* Truth:** God has given me three daughters-in-law and six granddaughters to love and who love me. I was blessed to have Rebekah for twenty years, and I will get to enjoy her for all eternity—with no failures on my part and with no friction.

> **little-*t* truth:** I failed to love my children well in countless ways. Things might be different today had I not failed so often. (Talk about a hope- and peace-killer!)
> **Big-*T* Truth:** God loves and has forgiven me. Rebekah loved and forgave me. My sons love and forgive me. God has and continues to change who I am! And I am able to minister in certain ways only because of my failures.

How about you?

> **little-*t* truth:** I have no idea how I will pay my bills.
> **Big-*T* Truth:** God is my Provider. God can make a way where there is no way. God promises to bless when I tithe.

> **little-*t* truth:** Look at the state of the world/country, the drug/sex trafficking, homelessness/poverty, inflation, anger, war, chaos, and so on.
> **Big-*T* Truth:** God is on His throne. He is calling me to be light in the darkness. I cannot "fix" the world, but I can, as God leads, bless those He brings across my path. I can give to trustworthy, Christ-centered missions and organizations.

I can choose not to engage in harsh, unkind arguments, whether in person or on social media.

little-*t* truth: I or a loved one has a devastating or unknown medical diagnosis.
Big-*T* Truth: Only God knows what the future holds, and He will be with me and/or my loved one every moment. He works all things for our good. Because I or my loved one knows Him, we will be healed either here or in heaven! I can choose to refuse to allow worry and fear of what lies ahead to rob me of joy right now.

little-*t* truth: My child or loved one is struggling. (Honestly, this is the hardest for me. I think it is because of my propensity to want to fix things, to "help" God, and not to want to wait on Him. It's also hard because we know that God will not force anyone to do anything and that sin has such devastating consequences.)
Big-*T* Truth: God hears my prayers. God is working. God loves my child or loved one infinitely more than I do! No one is too far for God's hand to reach. God can work in me as I lift my loved one up to Him. I can ask God to work in me and reveal to me how to love my child or loved one well.

Think on what is true, but be sure to apply the rest of the verse! Make sure it's Big-*T* Truths you're meditating on. Focus on, proclaim aloud, rehearse, and repeat the Truth. If you find yourself "stuck" on a truth that does not fit the other criteria, don't refuse to live in reality, but remind yourself that little-*t* truths must bend to Big-*T* Truths. Big-*T* Truths usurp little-*t* ones every time.

Chapter 21
Encouragement

Our last word to help us stay anchored to hope in God is *encouragement*. God walks with us to encourage us. He also asks us to encourage one another.

How do we allow God to encourage us? Again, through His Word! As I wrote that, the thought came to mind that there is nothing we need or deal with that the Word of God cannot help us with. That includes when we are feeling hopeless and discouraged.

Discouragement is like a fertilizer for hopelessness. Rehearsing, rehashing, and coddling—nurturing an unhealthy way—discouragement is like Miracle-Gro. The reality is that life can be brutal, unfair, and relentless in its negative, destructive impacts upon our bodies, finances, families, dreams, marriages, emotions, and mental well-being. Thus, discouragement is something we need to know how to address, or we will sooner or later be drowning in it.

Discouragement is not eliminated by a refusal to live in reality. It does not disappear by putting on a "happy face" or wearing spiritual spandex. If we try to conform to expectations (from ourselves or others), to refuse to acknowledge our difficulties, losses, and struggles, to project an image of "Super Faith," we are not accepting reality.

The Psalms feature great examples of times when the psalmist needed to encourage himself, but they never include a denial of reality. The psalms are brutally honest.

After my abdominal surgery, I had a vicious case of *C. difficile*. It was dreadful. While on staff at my church, I had prayed for people afflicted with *C. diff*. But after fighting it myself, I felt like I needed to go back to each one of those dear people because I had not prayed hard enough! Not only was I close to being referred to the CDC, but even after the toxin cleared, my intestinal tract was severely damaged.

I'm coming up on two years since my surgery, and I am still trying to heal my GI tract. This has been exceptionally discouraging. To be completely transparent, I'm uncomfortable when people ask me how I'm doing. I feel like I either have to lie or say I'm still struggling. I am doing better than I was; it's just taking time.

Who is going to encourage us if we are not honest? Who is going to know to check in, send a card or text message, or bring us a meal, let alone pray for us, if we are not transparent about our needs? Furthermore, how can we expect God to minister to us if we will not humble ourselves and admit to Him what He already knows? "I'm so discouraged, Lord! Please help me!"

Several months ago, I started having issues with my right thumb. When it worsened, I knew I needed to see a doctor, so I made an appointment with an orthopedist. He immediately recognized that the issue was with the tendon that runs along the edge of the inner wrist. He prescribed a high dose of an anti-inflammatory, hoping it would do the trick and wanted to see me again in three months. Unfortunately, the anti-inflammatory provided minimal relief. What it did do was greatly upset my stomach. So I quit taking it.

When I returned for the follow-up, I was asked, "How are you doing?" What would have happened if I had said, "Just great—that medication worked wonders"? They would have closed my chart, patted me on the shoulder, and said they were so happy for me. (And there would have been the tempting perk of no injection!)

Instead, I explained that the issue had gotten worse. At this point, my whole arm and shoulder hurt. I could not do anything at all with my right hand that did not hurt and had even quit using the electric toothbrush the dentist recommended; it was heavy enough that I couldn't hold it without severe pain. (I did try using my left hand, but it did not go very well.) I wasn't complaining to get attention. I knew that if I was not honest, I wouldn't get the help I needed.

So honest I was, and two weeks after the cortisone injection (which I would much prefer to never experience again), I was almost completely pain-free! Now I can do anything and everything once again with my right hand with zero pain. And my arm and shoulder are great too! (I had been protecting my hand so much that it was causing pain in my arm. Once my hand was fixed, the whole arm got better.)

This may sound like a repeat of our discussion on being open, and in a way, it is. But the point remains that encouragement in times of storms is crucial to our mental, emotional, and spiritual well-being. And the only way to receive the encouragement we need is to be honest about our need for encouragement.

For years after Rebekah's death, I sent weekly emails to a mighty group of prayer warriors, updating them on everything from the trial progress to God's faithfulness and what the Lord was teaching me. I would share honestly with this group from time to time (quite frequently during the first several years) that my grief was almost unbearable.

Later, I would be transparent on Facebook when I was having a spell of unrelenting, paralyzing grief. In both cases, in the days after sharing, a huge relief would come. Why? My situation had not changed. In fact, sometimes it would actually worsen, especially when it had to do with the justice system. Nothing had changed, but I was receiving the benefits of the prayers of friends and family who were warring on my behalf! It is vital that we reach out for encouragement when we can't encourage ourselves.

God walks with us to encourage us. He does this through His Spirit, who lives in us. He encourages supernaturally. Often, He does it through other people led by His Spirit.

One way God encourages us is when we praise Him. Music is a powerful tool that has a unique ability to speak to our souls, even without words. With words, that ability is magnified. Having songs to listen to, even if you are unable to sing the words, is a great way to lift God up, to refocus, and to remind ourselves of the Big-T Truths: who God is, who we are in Christ, how faithful God is, how loved we are, and so on.

It is my deep hope that you will take the time to listen to the songs I've shared at the back of this book. Let them minister to your soul. Let them remind you of what you already know about God. Become so familiar with them that you awaken with them in your mind and on your tongue. I've included a variety, and I understand that not everyone is going to like all of them. But give them a shot. If you don't care for one, simply move on to the next. Some are slow, and some are loud and upbeat. I find that I need both at different times — there is no formula.

When I'm really down, I sometimes need to listen to a quieter song — for my crying can be strong enough that I literally cannot sing — knowing that the words and melody are ministering to my soul. Other times, when just as down, I have gravitated toward more upbeat songs, letting their truths and energy pull me up.

You can find a Christian radio station you like and make your own list. I will say that during my times of deepest grief and struggle, there were some songs I couldn't listen to on the radio. They were great songs full of Truth, but instead of ministering, they somehow caused deeper pain and grief. So do what's best for you. We are all different, but I strongly urge you to immerse yourself in Christian music that feeds your soul with Truth, includes Scripture (making it easier to memorize), and encourages your heart to keep on hoping in Jesus.

After Rebekah's death, I must admit that I did not enjoy singing at church. It seemed that all I had to do was walk into the sanctuary when the music started playing, and I would immediately be in tears. And I don't mean gentle, softly flowing tears. I mean *ugly* tears. My pastor explained that in worship, we let our guards down, so to speak. We relax enough that tears held at bay begin to flow. But God meets us in those tears! So do not stifle them or avoid worship.

Let me make one other point before we leave the subject of praise. In Hebrews 13:15, the writer speaks of the "sacrifice of praise": "Therefore, let us offer through Jesus a continual sacrifice of praise to God, proclaiming our allegiance to his name."

And in Psalm 50:14–15, the author speaks of making "thankfulness your sacrifice":

> Make thankfulness your sacrifice to God,
> and keep the vows you made to the Most High.
> Then call on me when you are in trouble,
> and I will rescue you,
> and you will give me glory.

Dear reader, when is praise a *sacrifice*? When is it *sacrificial* to offer thanksgiving to God? Not when things are going well! At these times, praise and thanksgiving flow from our hearts and mouths with ease. It is not hard to be thankful when we are experiencing life to its fullest. It is not hard to offer praise when we can see clearly how good God is and all the good He does in our hearts and lives!

Praise and thanksgiving become a sacrifice only when our hearts are heavy. Only when we are struggling. Only when difficulties and darkness and pain obscure the loving hand of God. Only when dire circumstances arise and the enemy plants seeds of doubt about the goodness of our heavenly Father. Only when—in spite of what we see, hear, experience, fear, grieve, and suffer—we lift our voices and our hands in praise and thanksgiving to the One True God is it a sacrifice!

God always delights in our praise and thanksgiving. *Always*. But can you imagine the depth of delight, of love, and of honor He experiences when our souls refuse to stop thanking and praising Him in the midst of heartache, tragedy, loss, neediness, and pain?

I had originally memorized Psalm 50:15 because of God's promise to rescue me and my desire to give Him all the glory when He does. But that word *then* became problematic to me.

Then means that something happens first—something that verse 15 is contingent upon. And when I looked it up . . . wow! God rescues us from trouble when we have made it a practice to thank Him in all circumstances and be obedient to His Word.

Now, God is immensely gracious and merciful. He does rescue when we do not deserve it. Even when it's our own failures, stubbornness, mistakes, and choices that land us in desperate need of rescue, He will show up. But if we want God to be attentive to our cries—if we want to be assured of His rescue in such a way that we have an indestructible rope to cling to—we must look at these two verses together.

Our choice to express thankfulness in difficulty or tragedy and our honest desire to always be obedient precipitate God's promise to rescue. Gratitude to God has great power when it is expressed through tears and with a broken heart. It is a reminder that we love, serve, and worship the Lord for who He is, not only for what He does for us. It is a declaration to the world and to the enemy of our souls that no matter what we are going through, we know God is good. There is an infinite amount of thankfulness and praise to offer Him, the Lover and Savior of our souls and the Giver of all good gifts!

I love the words Dane Ortlund shares in his book, which I've already quoted, *Gentle and Lowly*:

> If you are in Christ, you have a Friend who, in your sorrow, will never lob down a pep talk from heaven. He cannot bear to hold himself at a distance. Nothing can hold him back. His heart is too bound up with yours.[13]

---

13. Ortlund, p. 50.

For many of us, it is praise and worship music that gives us a glimpse into His heart, an understanding of, if not actually physically felt, His ever-present closeness. Try it. If you struggle, set it aside and come back later to try it again. But do not allow your difficulty in *singing* praise keep you from *speaking* words of gratitude and praise to the Lord. Thankfulness and praise are great ways to lift our eyes off ourselves and our circumstances and fix them on Jesus.

VI.
Triumph

Chapter 22
Our Choice

In his book *An Eye for Miracles*, Dr. Paul Risser reflects on the Lord's response to Sarah in Genesis 18, when she was told at ninety years of age that she would bear a son—"Is anything too hard for the Lord?"—and Jesus's words in Luke 18:27: "The things that are impossible with men are possible with God." Dr. Risser shares this encouraging outline (the words in brackets are mine):

- No sickness is too bad that God cannot heal it. [And we can hope/pray for healing.]
- No storm is so turbulent that He cannot calm it. [And we can hope/pray for peace.]
- No giant is so large that He cannot conquer him. [And we can hope/pray for giants to fall.]
- No mountain is so big that He cannot bring it down. [And we hope/pray for mountains to be made flat in the name of Jesus.]
- No financial crisis is so severe that He cannot remedy it. [And we can hope/pray for provision.]
- No relationship is so broken that He cannot mend it. [And we can hope/pray and do all in our power for relational healing.]

But the truth is that, in this world, there are times when healing does not come, storms are not calmed, giants do not fall but continue to terrorize, mountains continue to be tremendous obstacles, needs are not met, and, worst of all in my opinion, relationships are not mended. What then?

Then we have a choice:

1. We can get angry with God, ourselves, and everyone else. We can accuse God of not caring, not loving, not seeing, not being able (in other words, accuse God of not being who He says He is). When we make this choice, we become bitter, angry, hopeless, destructive, and—may I be honest and say—ungodly people.
2. Or we can declare aloud and believe with all our hearts another point in Dr. Risser's outline:

- No disappointment is so overwhelming that He cannot redeem it.

Praise God for this truth! When all our "hope-fors" lie in ashes at our feet, our heart is crushed, and it seems that darkness has won, we stand naked before our God, stripped of all our positive thinking, all our efforts to control, all our grand illusions of a carefree existence on this earth, all our pride and self-righteousness and pretense. We lay our masks and our boxes and our dreams and our hope-fors at the feet of Jesus. And we lift trembling, weary, bruised hands and tear-filled, bloodshot, swollen eyes and praise our God who is so powerful that He can redeem all—*all*—things!

And then, we bow in surrender to our God, who is *utterly* good and whose plans for us are nothing but good. God who is, even now—perhaps *especially* now—faithful and true, full of compassion and mercy and grace, and who can give us beauty unimaginable for the ashes of our hope-fors. God who weeps for and with us, His beloved children, who are suffering.

Our choice is actually quite simple: Do we run from our misperception of who God is? Or do we run into the arms of the only *One* in whom we can place our hope and never be disappointed?

The first option leads to a lifetime in the pit of despair, surrounded by the ashes of our dreams, filled with hopelessness, and under the crushing abuse of Satan.

The second option leads us to a good, good Father who will reach down and lovingly, gently lift us up out of that pit of despair. He will steady us as we walk a little farther from that pit every day, and He will lift us out again when we fall back in. He will give us a brand-new song to sing. A different song, of which we might desire different lyrics, but a beautiful song nonetheless!

It tells others of God's faithfulness. It is honest enough to be sung through tears, allowing the audience to see our ashes so they know we can relate to them and theirs. Yet, despite the tears, it is sung with a radiant face that reflects the joy in our hearts in reaction to the goodness, faithfulness, and immeasurable love of God. This song allows them to "taste and see that the Lord is good" (Psalm 34:8), that they may trust in our good, good God too!

Hebrews 10:23 (emphasis mine): "Let us *hold tightly without wavering* to the hope we affirm, because *God can be trusted to keep His promises*."

Our ability to trust in God—His goodness, faithfulness, power, and promises as well as His ability to transform us and redeem all things—is why we can be people of hope!

Romans 15:13: "I pray that God, the source of hope, will fill you completely with joy and peace because you trust in Him. Then you will overflow with confident hope through the power of the Holy Spirit."

On August 21, 2013, a young man entered an elementary school in Georgia with a high-powered rifle and 500 rounds of ammunition. His goal was to kill as many people as possible before he was taken down.

In the school office, where he entered to begin his bloody rampage, was a woman by the name of Antoinette Tuff. She was a school bookkeeper—an ordinary person just like you and me. Over the next twenty minutes or so, Antoinette interacted with this young man.

He did fire on the police, and they fired back, but the event ended without any loss of life or bodily harm to anyone that day, thanks to Antoinette's intervention. She is without a doubt a true heroine, but, as all true heroes, she is also humble, crediting her faith in God and being anchored in Him for her success that day.

How in the world does an ordinary woman talk a gunman intent on mass murder into complete surrender? Antoinette offered the man the following:

- Respect: She called him "sir" repeatedly.
- Love: She said she loved him.
- Worth: She told him she was proud of him.

These are all wonderful, important things, but I want to focus on something else she offered him. The gunman walked into that school and Antoinette's office loaded with ammo but totally void of one of the most basic necessities of a productive life:

Hope.

He had no hope. He shared his despair with Antoinette, his belief that his life was meaningless and beyond redemption. And she, in turn, offered him hope. In an interview afterward, she said, "I wanted to allow him to know there was some hope." Hope that his life could get better. Hope that it was not too late for him to stop what he had started. Hope for the future as well as for the moment.

How many people do we come into contact with who are just like that young man? They may not be toting a gun, but they may be just as devoid of hope.

My fervent prayer is that we will experience the hope we have in Christ in the midst of our storms and that we will be able to share that hope with others. We will have the opportunity to share that we too have been stuck in pits. Some of our own making, some because of others, some because we live in a fallen world, and some because life is not fair or just or easy. But by God's grace and help, we found and still cling to hope. And we tell others that they can too.

Chapter 23
The Pathway to Peace

The Serenity Prayer
By Reinhold Niebuhr (1892–1971)

God, grant me the serenity to accept the things I cannot change;
The courage to change the things I can,
And the wisdom to know the difference.
Living life one day at a time, enjoying one moment at a time,
Accepting hardship as the pathway to peace.
Taking, as Jesus did, this sinful world as it is, not as I would have it;
Trusting that He will make all things right if I surrender to His will.
That I might be reasonably happy in this life,
And supremely happy with Him forever in the next.

At first glance, this may seem an odd prayer to include in a book about hope. But I believe that if we look closely at it, we will find it is quite appropriate.

First, let's recognize that hope and peace are, like hope and trust, irrevocably linked. There is no hope where there is no peace, and vice versa. Now, read it again; I pray that it is anointed and effective in helping you, and that you, like me, might want to memorize it.

I believe it is a great follow-up to our litany of humility. Accepting things we can't change and changing things we can both take humility. It takes humility to embrace that we are not God but that there are things we need to change. Ninety-nine percent of the time, I believe those things that need to change are found within us. For ourselves are just about the only things we can change. Sometimes we can change our circumstances: change jobs, eat better, retire, seek new friends, change what we listen to/watch/read, and so on. But there are many more circumstances we cannot change.

My daddy always said that the only thing we can always choose (and thus always change) is our attitude. Having an attitude of accepting what we cannot change, being positive, extending mercy, allowing God to work in the fiery furnaces we find ourselves in leads to peace.

Having the courage to address things, even difficult things, that we can and should change, leads (eventually) to peace. Although the going can be tough, once we get to the other side, we will find relief and joy in whatever change God enabled us to accomplish.

The wisdom to know the difference means not immersing ourselves in worry, or trying to manipulate or manage, or being in constant inner turmoil and sorrow over those things we cannot change. This leads to wonderful rest and peace.

Living life one day at a time means staying in the present. Again, not looking back in regret or ahead in fear, but simply finding joy in our present moment with a grateful heart. We accept that hardship is a part of life in this sinful, fallen world—a world that is no different than what Jesus experienced.

Jesus walked a harder path than you and I will ever have to walk (all because He chose to walk it for us) and was victorious. The same Holy Spirit that lived in Him lives in you and me, and we can be victorious as well. For if we surrender to His will, at some point—tomorrow, next month, in twenty years, or when we stand before Him in our brand-new, immortal bodies—He will make all things right and new. This brings much peace to those of us who have suffered injustice, unfairness, and premature loss.

Lastly, it brings peace when we do not expect supreme happiness in this world. We can have peace in the gratitude for and the enjoyment of the reasonable happiness we experience here, while we look forward with certain hope to the supremely happy future God has planned for all of us who will dwell with Him forever.

When our hope-fors crash and burn, it's okay to grieve. It's okay to mourn the loss of something, even if it is only a dream. It's even okay to ask why.

It's okay to ask God questions. I know this is true for several reasons: (1) God did not rebuke people in the Bible for asking questions. (2) How can we learn if we do not ask questions? And (3), on a personal level, when I asked God if He had heard my prayers for Rebekah, He answered me.

But when asking questions, keep these points in mind:

1. You can ask God anything you want. But you may not demand that He answers you.

2. Ask God questions from a position that acknowledges that He is God and you are not. Embody an attitude of respect and humility.
3. You must accept that there are things you will not know, understand, or have answers to here on earth. God's ways are far higher than ours. His thinking is far above our own. Besides, as someone once said, would we want a God that we could understand? Talk about limiting God!

As an aside, I know there are people who say they will ask God this or that when they get to heaven. Perhaps they will, but I don't think so. I think many of our questions that we long to have answered are born and nurtured from a place of limited faith, limited understanding of God's character, and limited knowledge of how the importance of eternity outweighs the here and now. I believe that once we are face to face with Jesus, when we are held in reverential awe of His goodness, compassion, mercy, and grace, we won't have any more questions to ask. Our questions will be broken apart and washed away in the massive tidal wave of our holy, holy, holy God, in whom there is no darkness:

> Now we see things imperfectly, like puzzling reflections in a mirror, but then we will see everything with perfect clarity. All that I know now is partial and incomplete, but then I will know everything completely, just as God now knows me completely (1 Corinthians 13:12).

4. If it seems like God is not answering your questions, you should release them and ask for help in asking different questions. My beloved pastor, Brandon Williams, always suggested that we stop asking, "Why?" and begin asking, "What?" *What do you want to teach me, Lord? What do You want to reveal about Yourself? What do You want to address and change in me?* Perhaps ask, "How?" *How do I walk through this in*

a way pleasing to You? How can I cooperate with You in this pit, Lord?

Think about the questions Zechariah and Mary asked Gabriel after each was told they would have a son. To Zechariah, Gabriel announced that he and his wife, Elizabeth, despite being well past their childbearing years, would have a baby boy who they were to name John. The archangel even told Zechariah that it was in answer to their prayers that this miraculous pregnancy would occur.

Zechariah's response came in the form of a question: "How can I be sure this will happen? I'm an old man now, and my wife is also well along in years" (Luke 1:18). His question came from his disbelief that God could do anything so late in the game. He could not be "sure" that God would do what the angel said. Zechariah was disciplined, not for his question but for his lack of belief. Although, he still received the promise!

(I'm so grateful that God loves us enough to discipline us and so much that He cannot go against who He is; He fulfills His every promise even when we do not deserve it.)

Compare his question to Mary's: "But how can this happen?" she asked the angel in Luke 1:34. "I am a virgin." Note the subtle difference: "How can this happen?" versus "How can I be sure this will happen?" Mary believed what Gabriel told her, but she was having a hard time wrapping her head around how God would accomplish such a thing. And rather than discipline, Mary received an answer, although I doubt that she, nor anyone since, can fully comprehend it.

I believe it pleases God greatly when, in our pit of despair — when surrounded by heartache and loss and broken dreams, when covered in the ashes of our deeply longed-for hopes and desires—we ask Him questions while at the same time taking Him at His word.

God knows our thoughts anyway. Why then would we try to hide our questions and doubts from Him? There is nothing wrong with the brutal, gut-wrenching honesty of crying out to God.

God, this is not what I wanted! This is not what I hoped and prayed for! I do not understand why You did not intervene the way I prayed. I cannot see how this is better. But in my grief, in my disappointment, in my confusion, in my anger, in my utter brokenness, I will trust You. I will believe even though I cannot see that You are with me. Though I cannot see that You were with my loved one. Though I cannot see that You have been working and will continue to work in this loss, injustice, betrayal, pain, grief, and lengthy suffering for my good and Your glory.

Help me, Lord! Help me stay true to You. Help me trust You. Help me look for Your hand of goodness and provision. Help me have a heart of gratitude and trust. Give me compassion through this trial. Help me cooperate with You so that I am more like Jesus. Help me be patient as I wait on You to do whatever it is that You are longing to do in me and for me and those I love. And help me place wrongs done to me or those I love in Your hands, not seeking vengeance but trusting You, even in this.

Right here, right now, in this pit, surrounded by these ashes, and plagued by these questions, I choose to join the author of Lamentations (3:21–24) in saying,

> Yet I still dare to hope
> when I remember this:
> The faithful love of the LORD never ends!
> His mercies never cease.
> Great is his faithfulness;
> his mercies begin afresh each morning.

I say to myself, "The LORD is my inheritance; therefore, I will hope in him!"

Epilogue

What if you've read through this whole book and you still have no hope? You can hope for other people but not for yourself—not in the situation you're in, not with so many cards stacked against you. What do you do now?

First, find someone you know who loves God, knows Him and His Word, and who loves you. This is someone who loves you enough to be honest with you, not just commiserate with you and excuse your feelings. Find that person who will not be cruel or judgmental or try to lecture you, who will not shame you or guilt you, but someone who will patiently and lovingly point you back again to the truths of who God is and what His Word says (as well as what it does not say). Humble yourself and share honestly where you are with this person. Ask them to pray for you. And should that person either join you in your hopelessness or judge and criticize you, thank them for their time and quickly find someone else.

Second, remind yourself of the truths in Scripture. Get back in God's Word! Read the Gospels, read Philippians, Romans, the Psalms. Or use the verses in the back of this book. Turn the verses into prayers. Meditate on and memorize your favorites. I remember declaring out loud and emphatically Psalm 42:11: "Why am I so discouraged? Why is my heart so sad? I will put my hope in God! I will praise him again—my Savior and my God." The *moment* you recognize that you are not experiencing peace and hope, but rather fear and doubt, examine your thoughts. Make sure your thinking is focused on Big-*T* Truths!

Third, start that gratitude journal, looking for things to thank the Lord for each day. And look closely for His hand in ways that are hidden. Remember: Every good gift comes from God the Father (James 1:17).

Fourth, you may need to repent of your own sin. Throughout this book, you have read about attitudes that are displeasing to God and lead to a place of hopelessness. Although they may seem unrelated, these sins will steal your hope: pride, unforgiveness, manipulation (of others or God), self-centeredness, wayward thoughts that are displeasing to God, not believing who God is—His goodness in particular. I'm sure you get the idea. These attitudes are wrong, not just because I say so but because God says so. And because they are wrong, they injure us. They cause harm to our souls, our relationships, and our faith. This is why God wants to free us from them.

Ask the Lord to examine your heart and point out anything that offends Him (Psalm 139:24). The Passion Translation of this psalm asks God to "see if there is any path of pain I'm walking on." This world is full of enough pain, wouldn't you agree? Let's not add to our suffering by choosing to embrace sin, no matter how "small" or tantalizing.

Fifth, examine very closely where your hope is. Is it in God, or in something/someone else, or in a certain outcome? Make sure that while you hope *for* things like healing, a better job, and restoration of relationships, your hope is firmly placed *in* God alone.

Lastly, dear reader: Hang in there! Do not allow the enemy to convince you that things will never change. *Things* may never change on this side of heaven, but *you* can change! You can allow God to work through these hopeless circumstances, pain, loss, grief, betrayal, divorce, and disease to make you more like Jesus, who is our "source of hope."

I recently had a friend who loves Jesus admit that she was utterly void of any hope for herself. She had become convinced that God did not want good things for her. Being on the outside, it was easy for me to recognize this as the enemy's voice. But in the midst of tremendous grief over the loss of a beloved parent, a child on the brink of suicide, worry for her grandchildren, and the dulled but ever-present sorrow over a failed marriage, miscarriages, poor health, and so on, well, that voice just sounded like fact.

As I grieved with her and for her, I tried to do what I have shared above: point her toward gratitude, God's faithfulness, God's Word, and the rest, with as much love and understanding as I could express through text messages. She was so gracious and receptive but remained adamant that while she could hope for other people, she could not hope for herself.

On the second or third day of our communications, during my quiet time, I read the story of Jesus feeding the four thousand. It's found in Mark 8, and as I read, I could picture my dear friend sitting in the presence of Jesus on a lovely, green hill. This is what I shared with her from Mark 8:1–13:

> About this time another large crowd had gathered, and the people ran out of food again. Jesus called his disciples and told them, "I feel sorry for these people. They have been here with me for three days, and they have nothing left to eat. If I send them away hungry, they will faint along the way. For some of them

have come a long distance..." So Jesus told all the people to sit down on the ground. Then he took the seven loaves, thanked God for them, and broke them into pieces. He gave them to his disciples, who distributed the bread to the crowd... They ate as much as they wanted.

I wrote the following:

> Jesus says this about you, His beloved child: "I feel such compassion for you. You have been with me all these years, and now you are depleted with nothing to nourish your soul."

His compassion for you is *great*! He will not send you away without "feeding" you! He knows that as long as we live on this earth, we are in desperate need of His sustenance. Oh, dear friend, I know you love the Word of God! Could it be that because of all your energy poured into [your loved one who was dying], because of a season of your heart being split between feasting on the Word and seeking to please [someone], because of the weight of tremendous concern for [loved ones], your soul has been malnourished in the Word? I've been there! And that is when we are the weakest, unable to fight effectively against the lies of the enemy that we would be able to recognize so easily at other times.

The important thing is that Jesus looks at you not with disgust or condemnation, not with disappointment or rejection... His eyes, His heart are filled with deep, deep compassion! Oh, how He loves us even when we falter!

The second important thing is to let Jesus feed you, dear one. Rest, eat food, drink water, *and* get in the Word! Feast on Truth! Truth about who God is, how He loves you, how faithful and kind and merciful He is. How we are told over and over again: we *will* have trouble in this world! But He is in us, and He has overcome the world and the evil one! We have heaven to look forward to! In the meantime, we navigate truly horrendous things, only sustained by His grace and His love. Our need can seem *so* great! So all-consuming. So endless and massive, we can be tempted to think that even Jesus cannot do/be all we need. But this too is a lie from the enemy. We are looking from a human perspective as the disciples did. We see a mass of problems, fears, concerns, needs, heartaches . . . over 4,000 men strong, plus women and children! But Jesus has enough! He has *more* than enough! He has enough to nourish you, and then several baskets of leftovers that you can share with others: [those loved ones you agonize over], coworkers[, etc.] in due season. You must feed yourself first! Let Jesus strengthen and restore you first.

Then I assured her of my continued prayers for her and her loved ones.

In my years as a biblical guidance director at my church, there were times when I met with people and, upon sharing some insight, direction, truth, compassion, or correction with them, I would know that what I spoke was not from me but from the Lord! It was too good, too spot on, too powerful, or too helpful to be *my* words. And I tried to always give credit to the Lord, saying, "I really believe that was from the Lord, not from me."

That is the way I felt about the above exchange with my friend. And that is why I wanted to include it here. I've read books and closed them after reading the last page, feeling defeated and chastised because I could not measure up to what the author either suggested or stated in so many words that God required of me. Don't get me wrong; God does require things of us. Hard, hard things! *But* His grace and mercy are great when we fall. His compassion is unlike anything we can imagine. And His love for us never wavers, although sometimes our choices stay His hand of blessing until we reposition ourselves under His authority and obey Him.

If you are still struggling with hopelessness, please know this: God sees you! He knows like no other the reason hope is so hard for you to grasp right now. He may know even better than you do. And He does not condemn you nor turn His back on you. He does not shake His head in disgust, and He is not frustrated with you. He is with you in that pit of despair. Right there beside you! He is patient, gentle, and kind. And He will never leave you or forsake you.

However, dear reader, He does not want you to remain in that pit. Do everything you can to help yourself, to "feed" yourself, and allow Him to do what you cannot. Determine to walk in obedience, to think on (dwell on) what is not only true but also conforms to the other qualifiers in Philippians 4:8, to get in the Word, to speak to your soul, to pick and choose from my suggestions, or to come up with your own.

And then trust that God will light up that dark pit! He will lift you out! He will steady you and help you as you walk in newfound hope, although your steps may be wobbly and faltering.

Psalm 18:28–29 says, "You light a lamp for me. The LORD, my God, lights up my darkness. In your strength, I can crush an army; with my God I can scale any wall."

Look for the tiny glimmers where His loving hands are intervening on your behalf, and choose to place your hope in Him alone. Ask God to help your hope grow. He longs to do this for you! Join the man in Mark 9:24 who saw Jesus bring hope and life to an utterly hopeless, lifeless situation but was first honest enough to say, "I do believe! Help me overcome my unbelief."

"Hope-Full" Scriptures

We Hope in *Who* God Is

PSALM 106:1
Praise the LORD! Give thanks to the LORD for He is good! His faithful love endures forever.

LAMENTATIONS 3:21–24
Yet I still dare to hope when I remember this: the faithful love of the LORD never ends. His mercies never cease. Great is His faithfulness: his mercies begin afresh each morning. I say to myself, "The LORD is my inheritance: therefore I will hope in him!"

JEREMIAH 29:11
"For I know the plans I have for you," says the LORD. "They are plans for good and not for disaster, to give you a future and a hope."

PSALM 25:8
The LORD is good and does what is right. . .

JAMES 1:17
Whatever is good and perfect is a gift coming down to us from

God our Father, who created all the lights in the heavens. He never changes or casts a shifting shadow.

PSALM 27:13
Yet I am confident I will see the LORD's goodness while I am here in the land of the living.

PSALM 25:4–5 NIV
Show me your ways, LORD, teach me your paths. Guide me in your truth and teach me, for you are God my Savior, and my hope is in you all day long.

PSALM 77:11–14
I will remember the deeds of the LORD; yes, I will remember Your miracles of long ago. I will meditate on all Your works and consider all Your mighty deeds. You ways, O God, are holy. What god is so great as our God? You are the God who performs miracles, You display Your power among the peoples.

Hope and Waiting

PSALM 5:3 NIV
In the morning, LORD, you hear my voice. In the morning I lay my requests before you and wait expectantly.

PSALM 62:5
Let all that I am wait quietly before God, for my hope is in him.

PSALM 37:7
Be still in the presence of the LORD and wait patiently for him to act.

ISAIAH 64:4
For since the world began, no ear has heard and no eye has

seen a God like you, who works for those who wait for him!

Psalm 46:10
Be still, and know that I am God.

Micah 7:7
As for me, I look to the Lord for help. I wait confidently for God to save me, and my God will certainly hear me.

Romans 8:24–25
We were given this hope when we were saved.

(If we already have something, we don't need to hope for it. But if we look forward to something we don't yet have, we must wait patiently and confidently.)

And finally, my favorite verse that I have turned to again and again:

John 5:17
Jesus replied, "My Father is always working, and so am I."

Trust Is the Foundation of Hope

Psalm 33:20–22
We put our hope in the Lord. He is our help and shield. In him our hearts rejoice, for we trust in his holy Name. Let Your unfailing love surround us Lord, for our hope is in you alone.

Romans 15:13
I pray that God, the source of hope, will fill you completely with joy and peace because you trust in Him. Then you will overflow with confident hope through the power of the Holy Spirit.

Isaiah 26:3–4
You will keep in perfect peace all who trust in You, all whose thoughts are fixed on You! Trust in the Lord always, for the Lord God is the eternal Rock.

Jeremiah 17:7
But blessed are those who trust in the Lord and have made the Lord their hope and confidence.

Hebrews 10:23
Let us hold tightly without wavering to the hope we affirm, for God can be trusted to keep his promises.

Isaiah 30:15
This is what the Sovereign Lord, the Holy One of Israel says, "Only in returning to me and resting in me will you be saved. In quietness and confidence is your strength. . ."

Psalm 91:1–2
Those who live in the shelter of the Most High will find rest in the shadow of the Almighty. This I declare about the Lord: he alone is my refuge, my place of safety; he is my God, and I trust him.

God Promises. . .

To be with us:

Isaiah 41:10
Don't be afraid, for I am with you. Don't be discouraged, for I am your God. I will strengthen you and help you. I will hold you up with my victorious right hand.

Zephaniah 3:17 (1984) NIV
The Lord your God is with you, he is mighty to save. He will

take great delight in you, he will quiet you with His love, he will rejoice over you with singing.

Deuteronomy 31:8 NIV
The Lord himself goes before you and will be with you; he will never leave you nor forsake you. Do not be afraid; do not be discouraged.

Isaiah 43:1–3
But now, O Jacob, listen to the Lord who created you. O Israel, the One who formed you says, "Do not be afraid for I have ransomed you. I have called you by name; you are mine. When you go through deep waters I will be with you. When you go through rivers of difficulty, you will not drown. When you walk through the fire of oppression you will not be burned up; the flames will not consume you. For I am the Lord your God, the Holy One of Israel, your Savior. . ."

(What does it mean to be ransomed by God? Colossians 1:13–14 says, "For [God] rescued us from the kingdom of darkness and transferred us into the kingdom of His dear Son, who purchased our freedom and forgave our sins.")

Psalm 23
The Lord is my Shepherd; I have all that I need. He lets me rest in green meadows; he leads me beside peaceful streams. He renews my strength. [He restores my soul.] He guides me along the right path, bringing honor to his name. Even when I walk through the darkest valley, I will not be afraid, for you are close beside me. Your rod and your staff protect and comfort me. You prepare a feast for me in the presence of my enemies. You honor me by anointing my head with oil. My cup overflows with blessings. Surely your goodness and unfailing love will pursue me all the days of my life, and I will live in the house of the Lord forever.

To help us:

Psalm 18:27–29
You rescue the humble, but you humiliate the proud. You light a lamp for me; the Lord my God lights up my darkness. In your strength I can crush an army; with my God I can scale any wall.

Psalm 40:1–3
I waited patiently for the Lord to help me, and he turned to me and heard my cry. He lifted me out of the pit of despair, out of the mud and the mire. He set my feet on solid ground and steadied me as I walked along. He has given me a new song to sing, a hymn of praise to our God. Many will see what he has done and be amazed. They will put their trust in the Lord.

Isaiah 40:27–31
O Jacob, how can you say the Lord does not see your troubles? O Israel, how can you say God ignores your rights? Have you never heard? Have you never understood? The Lord is the everlasting God, the Creator of all the earth. He never grows weak or weary. No one can measure the depths of his understanding. He gives power to the weak and strength to the powerless. Even youths will become weak and tired, and young men will fall in exhaustion. But those who trust in the Lord will find new strength. They will soar high on wings like eagles. They will run and not grow weary. They will walk and not faint.

Nehemiah 8:10
. . .[T]he joy of the Lord is your strength!

Psalm 25:4–5
Show me the right path, O Lord; point out the road for me to follow. Lead me by your truth and teach me, for you are the

God who saves me. All day long I put my hope in you.

To redeem us:

Isaiah 61:1–2
The Spirit of the Sovereign Lord is upon me, for the Lord has anointed me to bring good news to the poor. He has sent me to comfort the brokenhearted and to proclaim that captives will be released and prisoners will be freed. He has sent me to tell those who mourn that the time of the Lord's favor has come, and with it the day of God's anger against their enemies. To all who mourn in Israel, He will give a crown of beauty for ashes, a joyous blessing instead of mourning, and festive praise instead of despair.

Romans 5:5 (1995) NASB
...[A]nd hope does not disappoint, because the love of God has been poured out within our hearts through the Holy Spirit who was given to us.

Romans 8:28
And we know that God causes everything to work together for the good of those who love God and are called according to his purpose for them.

Psalm 147:3 NIV
He heals the brokenhearted and binds up their wounds.

What Am I to Do?

1 Thessalonians 5:16–18
Always be joyful. Never stop praying. Give thanks in all circumstances for this is God's will for you who belong to Christ Jesus.

PSALM 42:11
Why am I so discouraged? Why is my heart so sad? I will put my hope in God! I will praise Him again—my Savior and my God!

ROMANS 12:12
Rejoice in our confident hope. Be patient in trouble. And keep on praying.

PSALM 50:14–15
Make thankfulness your sacrifice to God, and keep the vows you made to the Most High. Then call on me when you are in trouble and I will rescue you, and you will give me glory.

PHILIPPIANS 4:6–8
Don't worry about anything; instead, pray about everything. Tell God what you need, and thank him for all he has done. Then you will experience God's peace, which exceeds anything we can understand. His peace will guard your hearts and minds as you live in Christ Jesus.

And now, dear brothers and sisters, one final thing. Fix your thoughts on what is true, and honorable, and right, and pure, and lovely, and admirable. Think about things that are excellent and worthy of praise.

PSALM 130:5
I am counting on the LORD; yes, I am counting on him. I have put my hope in his word.

While James is my favorite book in the New Testament, I have said that if I were stranded on a deserted island and could only have one chapter of the Bible to read, it would be Romans 8. To me, it sums up the whole message of the Gospel. I have memorized it and so very often find myself sharing specific verses with others and reciting it to myself.

Romans 8

So now there is no condemnation for those who belong to Christ Jesus. And because you belong to him, the power of the life-giving Spirit has freed you from the power of sin that leads to death. The law of Moses was unable to save us because of the weakness of our sinful nature. So God did what the law could not do. He sent his own Son in a body like the bodies we sinners have. And in that body God declared an end to sin's control over us by giving his Son as a sacrifice for our sins. He did this so that the just requirement of the law would be fully satisfied for us, who no longer follow our sinful nature but instead follow the Spirit.

Those who are dominated by the sinful nature think about sinful things, but those who are controlled by the Holy Spirit think about things that please the Spirit. So letting your sinful nature control your mind leads to death. But letting the Spirit control your mind leads to life and peace. For the sinful nature is always hostile to God. It never did obey God's laws, and it never will. That's why those who are still under the control of their sinful nature can never please God.

But you are not controlled by your sinful nature. You are controlled by the Spirit if you have the Spirit of God living in you. (And remember that those who do not have the Spirit of Christ living in them do not belong to him at all.) And Christ lives within you, so even though your body will die because of sin, the Spirit gives you life because you have been made right with God. The Spirit of God, who raised Jesus from the dead, lives in you. And just as God raised Christ Jesus from the dead, he will give life to your mortal bodies by this same Spirit living within you.

Therefore, dear brothers and sisters, you have no obligation to do what your sinful nature urges you to do. For if you live by its dictates, you will die. But if through the power of the Spirit you put to death the deeds of your sinful nature, you will live. For all who are led by the Spirit of God are children of God.

So you have not received a spirit that makes you fearful slaves. Instead, you received God's Spirit when he adopted you as his own children. Now we call him, "Abba, Father." For his Spirit joins with our spirit to affirm that we are God's children. And since we are his children, we are his heirs. In fact, together with Christ we are heirs of God's glory. But if we are to share his glory, we must also share his suffering.

Yet what we suffer now is nothing compared to the glory he will reveal to us later. For all creation is waiting eagerly for that future day when God will reveal who his children really are. Against its will, all creation was subjected to God's curse. But with eager hope, the creation looks forward to the day when it will join God's children in glorious freedom from death and decay. For we know that all creation has been groaning as in the pains of childbirth right up to the present time. And we believers also groan, even though we have the Holy Spirit within us as a foretaste of future glory, for we long for our bodies to be released from sin and suffering. We, too, wait with eager hope for the day when God will give us our full rights as his adopted children, including the new bodies he has promised us. We were given this hope when we were saved. (If we already have something, we don't need to hope for it. But if we look forward to something we don't yet have, we must wait patiently and confidently.)

And the Holy Spirit helps us in our weakness. For example, we don't know what God wants us to pray for. But the Holy Spirit prays for us with groanings that cannot be expressed in words. And the Father who knows all hearts knows what the Spirit is saying, for the Spirit pleads for us believers in harmony with God's own will. And we know that God causes everything to work together for the good of those who love God and are called according to his purpose for them. For God knew his people in advance, and he chose them to become like his Son, so that his Son would be the firstborn among many brothers and sisters. And having chosen them, he called them to come to him. And having called them, he gave them right standing with himself. And having given them right standing, he gave them his glory.

What shall we say about such wonderful things as these? If God is for us, who can ever be against us? Since he did not spare even his own Son but gave him up for us all, won't he also give us everything else? Who dares accuse us whom God has chosen for his own? No one—for God himself has given us right standing with himself. Who then will condemn us? No one—for Christ Jesus died for us and was raised to life for us, and he is sitting in the place of honor at God's right hand, pleading for us.

Can anything ever separate us from Christ's love? Does it mean he no longer loves us if we have trouble or calamity, or are persecuted, or hungry, or destitute, or in danger, or threatened with death? (As the Scriptures say, "For your sake we are killed every day; we are being slaughtered like sheep.") No, despite all these things, overwhelming victory is ours through Christ, who loved us.

And I am convinced that nothing can ever separate us from God's love. Neither death nor life, neither angels nor demons, neither our fears for today nor our worries about tomorrow—not even the powers of hell can separate us from God's love. No power in the sky above or in the earth below—indeed, nothing in all creation will ever be able to separate us from the love of God that is revealed in Christ Jesus our Lord.

I used Scripture as a basis for the following prayers during one of my darkest times. It helps me to know I am praying according to God's will and to keep me from instructing Him! It also makes it easier for me to hear what He is telling me about me.

1 Peter 5:5–10:
I will place over myself, like the apron of a slave, humility toward others because I desire Your grace, God. You will give me grace if I am humble, but if I am proud, You will resist me. I will humble myself and bow in submission to Your mighty hand: I will trust You to do what is best; I will place _____ in Your hands and leave _____ there. I will throw all my cares upon You because You care for me, and I can rest knowing You will take care of this situation.

I will be self-controlled and on guard for Satan's attacks. I will recognize his lies by holding them up to the Word of God, and I will resist him by standing firm in my faith in Your ability to keep Your promises. I will remember those who are facing the same kinds of trials I am, and I will pray for them as I ask them to pray for me.

I will praise You, God, for You promise that You *will* restore my soul; You will make me strong, firm, and steadfast. You, O God, are all powerful and I will praise Your name forever! Amen.

Proverbs 3:5–7:
O Lord, help me trust You with all my heart concerning every detail of _____. Help me not try to figure things out on my own—help me not interfere with the work You are doing. Help me not become discouraged because of the way things appear to me but to praise You for the work You are doing that is as yet unseen. Help me in every way to be obedient to You, Lord. Help me seek to do Your will and trust that You will show me what Your will is. And, Lord, help me die to self and walk in obedience to You so that You can bless me. Help me remember that I do not know what is best—You do! And help me fear You enough to obey You even when I, in my flesh, would rather do my own thing. Help me avoid evil, Lord. And

help me recognize that when my way is not Your way, my way is evil. Help me humble myself, Lord, and choose Your way.

2 Corinthians 4:16–18:
I will not sink into despair and give up. Instead of looking at my circumstances, I will focus on Christ. Instead of drowning in grief over _____, I will focus on what God wants to do in my own heart and life. I will remember that these troubles will pass, but that the work God is doing in me will not only be greater than my grief, but it will also last forever. Again: I will not focus on what is seen, for it will not last. I will focus on the unseen for it is eternal.

Philippians 1:9–11:
O Lord! I pray that love will overflow more and more in _____'s heart. I pray for opportunities for them to grow in the knowledge *and* the understanding of who You are and Your Word so that they can understand what really matters, Lord. So they can focus on the eternal rather than the temporal. Fill them with the desire to live a pure and blameless life, Lord, and empower them to do so through Your Holy Spirit. I pray that they will be filled with the fruit of their salvation, the righteous character [you can list specifics such as honesty, sobriety, humility, etc.) produced in their life by Jesus Christ. May their life bring glory to You, God!

(This is a great prayer to pray for ourselves as well!)

You can take other verses and write your own prayers here:

Songs of Hope

Scan the QR code above to find a playlist that features the following music videos:

"Even If" by MercyMe

"Rest in You" by All Sons & Daughters

"Desperate" by Jamie MacDonald

"No Fear" by Jon Reddick and We the Kingdom

"Way Maker" by Leeland

"Crowns Down" by Gateway Worship

"Promises" by Maverick City Music

"Gratitude" by Brandon Lake

"I Will Carry You" by Ellie Holcomb

"Same God" by Elevation Worship

"Raise a Hallelujah" by Bethel Music

"Is He Worthy?" by Maverick City Music

"We Crown You" by Jeremy Riddle

"Peace in the Storm" by Ore Clarke

"Isaiah Song" by Maverick City Music

"Ever Be" by Bethel Music

"Word of God Speak" by MercyMe

"Hallelujah Even Here" by Lydia Laird

"Trust in You" by Lauren Daigle

"I Speak Jesus" by Charity Gayle

"Into the Sea (It's Gonna Be OK)" by Tasha Layton

"King of My Heart" by Kutless

"Rescue" by Jordan St. Cyr

"Still Waters (Psalm 23)" by Leanna Crawford

"There's Nothing That Our God Can't Do" by Passion Music

"Graves into Gardens" by Elevation Worship
"Still Standing" by Josh Baldwin

"Rescue" by Lauren Daigle

"Hold on to Me" by Lauren Daigle

"Look Up, Child" by Lauren Daigle

"Come Alive (Dry Bones)" by Lauren Daigle

"Peace Be Still" by the Belonging Co.

"Praise" by Elevation Worship

"Eye of the Storm" by Ryan Stevenson

"Running with You in the Dark" by Tenth Avenue North

"The Reminder" by TAYA

"Hallelujah Anyway" by Rend Collective

"Jesus, Lover of My Soul" by Awakening Music

Holding Hope in the Silence

When we come to a place of desperation—when despite our prayers, the prayers of others, the speaking aloud of God's Word, the genuine determination to hold on to the truth about who God is—we seem to be met with silence: no visible evidence that God is working on our behalf, on the behalf of those we love, or in the midst of the situation we are lifting up to Him... What do we do then?

As I again cried out on behalf of a loved one, the thought came that perhaps there comes a time when we stop praying for "this" and begin praying for "that." When healing, restoration, deliverance, provision, open doors, reunion, ease of pain/grief—whatever we have been pleading with the Lord for in the name of Jesus—does not come, we stop praying for *this* aspect of a situation or *this* particular desire of our heart.

We do not stop from a place of giving up! This is not giving up on God or on His ability to work! Rather, it is a place of surrendering *completely* to the Almighty God this thing that He *knows* we desire. It is trusting that He will not forget it or lay it aside carelessly. It is trusting that God is good and has good things for you. Period. No matter what changes do or do not happen. No matter whether our specific prayer is answered here on earth or in eternity.

We can approach the Lord from a place of woundedness and humility that cries, "I'm going to stop asking You for 'this,' Lord. I trust that You know my heart even when I do not ask. I trust that You will not forget my cries and my desires. But right now, I am going to place this desire/this plea/this concern/this heartache into Your hands, and I am going to surrender and rest from the weight of constantly bringing it before You, at least for a season. And as I place 'this' into Your all-powerful and loving hands, I am going to begin to ask You to help me cooperate with You in the waiting. I am asking You to help me cooperate with what You want to do within me in this place of difficulty. Work for my good, as You promise, while I am in this place I do not want to be, Father."

When we stop asking for "this" and begin asking for "that," it is not a lack of faith! It is, rather, an extraordinary, even supernatural display of faith in a good, good Father who promises to withhold no good thing from His children. It is not a losing of hope. It is placing all hope in the One who will never disappoint us. It is not a lackadaisical existence. But it is a focus on what awaits us in heaven for all eternity.

It is not a gray place of happenstance or a decision to just accept what is. It is a deliberate stepping into a place of peace, joy, and contentment, no matter our circumstances. It is embracing what we can control (which is actually an extremely small amount): our attitudes, our priorities, our responses, our tongues (although we cannot tame the tongue, and control only comes about through the Holy Spirit within us), our focus. And it is surrendering what we cannot control, which is pretty much everything else.

No matter what prayers, longings, desires, hopes, and dreams we find unfulfilled in this life, we can be filled with hope. That God is for us and not against us. That God is working, even in the awful, on our behalf. That we, if we are following Jesus, are being transformed ever more into His likeness. And that even if our circumstances do not change this side of heaven, we have all eternity to look forward to a time when everything — every single thing — will be good and perfect and we will never suffer in any way again.

We can entrust our deepest cries to the Lord. We can know that the Holy Spirit is lifting these cries to the Father with groanings that cannot be expressed in words and that He is pleading on our behalf — even when we lay those very cries at His feet in order to make space for Him to accomplish what has been obscured by our obsession (for lack of a better word) over what we have been bringing to Him. It removes the telescopic vision of what we do not perceive God is doing and opens our vision to all the ways He is working in and around and through us.

By not praying for "this" and instead praying for "that," we entrust God with "that" so He is free to do "this," which He knows carries eternal weight and will benefit us for all eternity. It is the focus on eternity that empowers, strengthens, and renews us day by day. It is this focus that brings encouragement in the place of discouragement. It is simply being obedient to God's command: "Be still, and know that I am God" (Psalm 46:10).

Recommended Reading

I am a reader! I love to read and have ever since I was a child. Perhaps it started when we lived in Germany; my parents could not afford to buy me a toy, but for twenty-five cents, they could afford a title in the Little Golden Books series, which would be enjoyed again and again. (Not only did I enjoy these books, but my children enjoyed and my grandchildren still enjoy several of them!)

I have books in every room of my house (except, strangely enough, the bathroom). Yes, even in the dining room, where I keep a basket that holds coloring books, crayons, and books that I read while the granddaughters color and we enjoy tea in the afternoon.

It was difficult to narrow down the titles that I feel have been most helpful to me. The process was somewhat helped by the fact that several are no longer in print. Just as with the songs I've chosen, not every book I recommend will be everyone's cup of tea. But I strongly encourage you to try one or two! Just read for at least a few minutes a day, along with the Bible, which is the most important book—whether we are happy or hopeless, flying high or in the pit of despair.

Jesus Calling: Enjoying Peace in His Presence (A 365-Day Devotional) by Sarah Young

I have read this book over and over and highly recommend it. It features a short devotional each day that uses Scripture to "speak" Jesus's heart to you.

One Thousand Gifts: A Dare to Live Fully Right Where You Are by Ann Voskamp

Ann Voskamp's writing is unique and captivating. She knows what it means to struggle and grieve, and she shares how important it is to find and give thanks to God for His wonderful gifts. I couldn't put this book down!

A Bend in the Road: Experiencing God When Your World Caves In by David Jeremiah

Doesn't the title say it all? With chapter titles that include: "Psalm for a Dark Night," "I Need Your Help, Lord," "Worship in Times of Trouble," "When You Are at Your Wits' End," "Triumph Over Trouble," and more, *A Bend in the Road* is a handbook of how to navigate times of great struggle and loss.

The 30-Day Praise Challenge by Becky Harling

Such a sweet, simple devotional that I can't recommend highly enough if you are struggling to praise the Lord or if you just want a refresher. Each day features a Scripture followed by an "Invitation," suggested songs to listen to, a prayer and a journal prompt.

Lastly, and not because it has anything to do with hopelessness, but because it is a book that can transform your life if you will read and apply it; because it is not only full of profound, clear truths that we somehow miss, but also of laugh-out-loud humor; because I think every single person should read this book; because when we are overwhelmed by storms we are more prone to offense; and because I'm the author of *this* book and get to recommend any book I want. . .

Unoffendable: How Just One Change Can Make All of Life Better by Brant Hansen

I have read this book four times, and need to read it again! Our world is so full of offense that we need to be on guard against it at all times. My copy is highlighted in many colors, underlined, asterisked, dog-eared, and notated. Read this book! You won't be sorry.

And now, not a book, but an engaging video course on forgiveness, available from Teach Every Nation:

70 x 7: Finding Peace by Forgiving Others and Yourself by Bruce Wilkinson

I believe hopelessness is sometimes an attack by the enemy of our souls. By that, I mean it's not just a result of hardship and grief but an outright demonic attack. I have absolutely experienced this myself, and a few times it was because of unforgiveness in my heart. Along with *Unoffendable*, I would love for every single person to go through this eight-video series.

Using remarkable stories, Bruce Wilkinson shares exactly what happens when we do not forgive others. He highlights Scriptures that we most likely know forwards and backwards and yet fail to grasp exactly what Jesus is saying. Watch, participate in the exercises, and experience profound freedom from the torturers!

I pray that this book I have written, the Scriptures and songs shared, and the extended reading suggestions will empower you to embrace the hope that is *yours* in Christ Jesus! Hope *in* God, no matter what you or your loved ones are experiencing right now because God is for you and in you and working on your behalf. He loves you and is oh, so very good! *And* we know the end of the story: We have eternity to look forward to where we will be "supremely happy" with God forever. In the meantime, watch for His loving hands as He blesses you along the most difficult path you are walking at this time. He *is* tenderly caring for you, His beloved.

www.ingramcontent.com/pod-product-compliance
Lightning Source LLC
Chambersburg PA
CBHW071213090426
42736CB00014B/2800